COMMONITORY FOR THE ANTIQUITY AND UNIVERSALITY OF THE CATHOLIC FAITH

OS JUSTI THEOLOGICAL CLASSICS
General Editor: Peter A. Kwasniewski

COMMONITORY
for
THE ANTIQUITY AND UNIVERSALITY OF THE CATHOLIC FAITH,
AGAINST THE PROFANE NOVELTIES OF ALL HERETICS

ST. VINCENT OF LÉRINS
Introduction by Alan Fimister

OS JUSTI PRESS

Os Justi Press
P.O. Box 21814
Lincoln, NE 68542
www.osjustipress.com

Send inquiries to
info@osjustipress.com

ISBN 978-1-965303-18-4 (paperback)
ISBN 978-1-965303-19-1 (hardcover)

Layout by Michael Schrauzer
Cover by Julian Kwasniewski
Cover image: Icon of the Synaxis of
the Venerable Fathers of Agaunum,
showing saints who lived at the
Abbey of St. Maurice in Switzerland,
founded by St. Sigismund in AD 515.
Wikimedia Commons.

CONTENTS

PREFACE

THE AUTHOR OF THE *COMMONITO-rium* was apparently a "late vocation" monk of Lérins Abbey on the Isle of Saint Honorat, off the coast of Nice in France. He wrote this work circa AD 434, about three years after the Council of Ephesus in 431; it is the only writing we have from him for sure. We don't know the exact date of his birth or his death, but he must have died before 450.

The word *commonitorium* signifies memorandum, aide-memoire, letter of instructions, a means of remembrance (from *commonitor*, one who earnestly reminds). Vincent appears to have written two commonitories but we have only one (see the end of chapter 28 and the summary in chapter 29). The second was to contain the testimonies of the holy fathers, i.e., the fathers of the Church prior to Vincent's time. Our author fell under the shadow of subscribing to Semipelagianism (against Augustine), but this has not interfered with veneration of him—he is mentioned in the *Roman Martyrology* on May 24—or lessened the great esteem in which his treatise has been held by later generations.

Vincent has no friendly feelings about new ideas and new doctrines. He speaks of "criminal novelties," "the rashness of profane novelty," "delight in the dirt of heretical novelty," and so forth; such candid rhetoric leaves little in doubt. Other things being equal, what is new is suspicious, what is old is trustworthy. Due to the "immutability of holy faith," "to announce to Catholic Christians a doctrine other than that which they have received was never permitted, is nowhere permitted, and never will be permitted," etc.; "nothing new is to be accepted; only what has been handed down by tradition." No wonder St. Vincent of Lérins has ever been a favorite source for Catholic traditionalists!

The *Commonitorium* poses the question: By what rule can we know doctrine to be sound? Here, Vincent famously articulates the Canon or Rule: "In the Catholic Church itself, every care should be taken to hold fast to what has been believed everywhere, always, and by all." Thus, the "confessors" at the time of the Arian crisis were able to stay faithful *because* they "stay[ed] in line with the decrees and definitions of all the priests of Holy Church as the heirs of Apostolic and Catholic Truth." In spite of the larger numbers ranged against them, they adhered to the Nicene Council of 325. Numbers do not matter; adherence to tradition alone matters. In pursuing this thesis, Vincent helpfully defines what the "consensus of the fathers" consists in—the criteria we should use for determining it. He defines the qualities of "a true and genuine Catholic" and contrasts them with the plight of those who run after novelties. One might say he offers a definition of modernism, 1,500 years *avant la lettre*: the desire to change or update religion, adding and subtracting according to private lights or fashionable beliefs.

But Vincent does still more. He explains why God allows eminent Catholics to go astray into error. His disquisition on the brilliant danger or dangerous brilliance of Origen could easily be translated into contemporary terms by substituting the name Hans Urs von Balthasar. He explains the way in which change is possible and desirable in the Church: there can and should be *profectus*—progress, success (from *proficiscor, proficisci*, to depart, set out, proceed)—but not *permutatio*, a substantial change or mutation into something else. He insists that any development must be compatible with what has come before, so that the later formulation may add, but may never contradict, the earlier. He instances the errors of Photinus, Apollinaris, and Nestorius, among others, as opportunities divinely given to the Church for clarifying and defending her own understanding of the two greatest mysteries of faith, the Trinity and the Incarnation: it was precisely these errors

that forced the Church to *formulate*, definitively, what was always held as the "apostolic and Catholic faith." In sum, for Vincent, your two best guides are council and consensus, i.e., the magisterium (which finds its highest expression in an ecumenical council) and the corporate witness of authentic teachers of the Faith.

"Truth comes by conflict," Hilaire Belloc once wrote. The truth may already be present, in the dense form of divine revelation, but the *formulation* required in order to respond to particular denials or distortions of that truth must be developed by the strenuous use of human intelligence aided by the gift of faith. Thus, terms like "Trinity, Incarnation, *Theotokos*" are not found in the New Testament, but what these terms signify *is* found in the New Testament or can be deduced from its premises. Perhaps one of the most striking aspects of the *Commonitorium* is the manner in which Vincent anticipates the Protestant principle of *sola Scriptura* and rejects it utterly, for, as he says, every heretic can find passages of Scripture with which to defend his position, but only the Catholic has a context into which every verse of Scripture fits, making coherent sense of them.

The modern reader wonders if Vincent offers us *fully adequate* criteria for distinguishing between orthodoxy and heresy. That is, just working with "ubique et semper et ab omnibus," and playing the one off the other in cases of doubt, can we be sure of discerning *clearly* the teaching that *most* accords with universality, antiquity, or consensus? When Vincent writes, "The Timothy of today is either, speaking generally, the Universal Church, or, in particular, the *whole body* of ecclesiastical superiors," it seems we are looking at an episcopal or conciliarist model. If there is no final authority in the Church, it is hard to see how certain issues could ever be resolved. Similarly, although Vincent provides criteria for the use of the testimonies of the Fathers, much later Peter Abelard's *Sic et Non* will show that the Fathers contradict one another on more than a few heads, thus raising doubts over the enterprise of dialectical

theology. The *consensus Patrum* can get you so far, but no farther. The possibility of erroneous applications of the Vincentian canon on the part of individual laymen, priests, or bishops, and the errancy of the Fathers in particular cases, loom on the horizon. It seems Vincent's canon would work only in two situations: where an inquirer knows *all* the sources that could provide relevant testimony for resolving a given controversy, which seems difficult, if not impossible — not least because the Fathers do not address every topic we may wish to know about, or some few might, but not most of them; or where there is a charism from God that *prevents* some member of the Church from falling into error in faith or morals. In the latter case, we would be looking at an authority that discerns, safeguards, and adequately expresses the essential universality, antiquity, and consent requisite for "apostolic and Catholic doctrine." To put it differently, we would want a sort of *living embodiment* of that doctrine, recognizable to all, so that confusion or disputes could ultimately be resolved. At this point, we have gone beyond the confines of Vincent's text, yet without rejecting the truth of his claims. A Catholic would say that Vincent is absolutely right as far as he goes, but that more is needed to fill out the ecclesiology.

When we look at the enormous historical influence of St. Vincent of Lérins — a major source for (*inter alia*) St. John Henry Newman, whom we might call "the Doctor of Development" — it is astonishing that the *Commonitorium* has not yet been published in a professionally typeset, bilingual, well-edited, and affordable format. Hitherto, one could find in booklet form an archaic English translation sloppily transcribed and clumsily laid out; a better edition is to hand if one is willing to plump for several Patristic works collected in one volume (yet still only in English); and one can find the Latin text by itself online, albeit with errata and lacunae. But a convenient Latin/English edition for use in the classroom or for private study has been unavailable until now.

The English translation contained herein was prepared by Rudolph E. Morris and published in 1949 by The Catholic University of America Press along with texts from Niceta of Remesiana, Sulpicius Severus, and Prosper of Aquitaine. This volume is now in the public domain. Scripture citations have been incorporated parenthetically into the body text throughout, to reduce the number of notes.

The Latin text contained here is the 1663 edition of Étienne Baluze (the "Baluziana"), as printed in the *Patrologia Latina* 50:637–86. I am grateful to my friend Dr. John Pepino for his painstaking work restoring the Latin text, fixing obvious typographical errors, making orthographic updates (e.g., *seculum* and *secularis* to *saeculum* and *saecularis*, *pene* to *paene*, *imo* to *immo*, *sigillatim* to *singillatim*, *tanquam* to *tamquam*), and filling a major lacuna. Dr. Pepino also corrected a few errors in the English translation.

The paragraphing is editorial.

The appendix, written by church historian Phillip Campbell, is taken from the site *Unam Sanctam Catholicam*, with permission.

Peter A. Kwasniewski
March 2, 2025
Quinquagesima Sunday

INTRODUCTION

by Alan Fimister[†]

LEO XIII DESCRIBED SACRED SCRIP-
ture as "a Letter, written by our heavenly Father,
and transmitted by the sacred writers to the human
race in its pilgrimage so far from its heavenly country."[1]
It is fitting, therefore, that St. Vincent of Lérins should
adopt in this work, which is essentially a guide to the
correct interpretation of Sacred Scripture, the pseud-
onym Peregrinus, the Latin for pilgrim (whence our word
peregrination).

At the very beginning of Our Lord's public ministry,
Jesus left Capharnaum:

> And in the morning, a great while before day, he
> rose and went out to a lonely place, and there
> he prayed. And Simon and those who were with
> him pursued him, and they found him and said
> to him, "Every one is searching for you." And he
> said to them, "Let us go on to the next towns,
> that I may preach there also; for that is why I
> came out." (Mark 1:35–38)

The word used here for "came out," ἐξῆλθον, is the same as
that used elsewhere (John 8:42) by Our Lord to describe
His eternal generation by the Father. Jesus's prayer, His
solitude, His eternal existence with God the Father and His
coming forth into the world to save sinners, his movement
from one town to the next in His public ministry—all are
a dwelling in and a sharing of His eternal "coming out"
of the Father and therefore also of His eternal breathing
forth of the Holy Spirit.

[†] Dr. Alan Fimister is Assistant Professor of Dogmatic Theology at Holy
Apostles College and Seminary in Cromwell, Connecticut.

[1] Leo XIII, *Providentissimus Deus* (1893), §1.

The ideal place, theretofore, in which to attempt this penetration of the sacred page is, Vincent explains, monastic seclusion.[2] The perfection of charity[3] is the proper context for divine reading, because it is through charity and not through some special expertise or secret knowledge that Our Lord makes known the depths of His word, impenetrable to the non-believer.

> Judas saith to him, not the Iscariot: Lord, how is it, that thou wilt manifest thyself to us, and not to the world? Jesus answered, and said to him: If any one love me, he will keep my word, and my Father will love him, and we will come to him, and will make our abode with him. (John 14:22–23)

Conversely, the absence of charity ensures the failure of the pilgrim's efforts to decipher the missives of our heavenly Father.

The correct starting place for the investigation of Christian doctrines for Vincent is always Scripture, but the Bible will not do on its own: "Holy Scripture, because of its depth, is not universally accepted in one and the same sense. The same text is interpreted differently by different people, so that one may almost gain the impression that it can yield as many different meanings as there are men."[4] And yet, it is important to observe that the examples St. Vincent then gives of the authors who so thoroughly contradict each other are all heretics: Novatian, Sabellius, Donatus, Arius, Eunomus, Macedonius, Photinus, Apollinaris, Priscillian, Jovinian, Pelagius, Celestius, and

---

[2] In his words (p. 5): "Far from the masses that overcrowd large cities, I am living in a very remote spot . . . within the cell of a monastery with nothing to distract me . . . . This way of life is well suited to the work I am planning to do."

[3] "That perfection of charity to which the counsels are directed . . . consists in man renouncing, as much as possible, temporal things, even such as are lawful, because they occupy the mind and hinder the actual movement of the heart towards God." *Summa theologiae* IIaIIae, Q. 44, art. 4, ad 3.

[4] Below, ch. 2, p. 9.

Nestorius. The implication is that Scripture truly is and would be "complete and more than sufficient in itself"[5] but for the malice of heretics.

So, Scripture, in normal circumstances is sufficient to establish any Christian doctrine but, as everyone knows, even the devil quotes Scripture, and his heretical satellites follow his example[6] when they "utter almost nothing of their own that they do not try to support with passages from the Scripture."[7] What, then, is the Christian to do, faced with this misuse of God's word? In one sense, he has no need to do anything, for, as St. John proclaims: "You have no need that any man teach you; but as his unction teacheth you of all things, and is truth, and is no lie. And as it hath taught you, abide in him" (1 John 2:27). The faithful Christian knows heresy when he hears it. On the other hand, he must be mindful of the stricture of St. Peter to be "ready always to satisfy every one that asketh you a reason of that hope which is in you" (1 Pet. 3:15). It is here, in taking up "the sword of the Spirit which is the word of God" (Eph. 6:17) against the novelties[8] of heretical depravity, that the pilgrim has need of Vincent's Canon to refute the enemies of the faith.

The so-called Vincentian Canon—namely, that the Christian should believe what has been held everywhere, always, and by everyone—is relatively well known. Unfortunately, it is too often received as a rather restrictive slogan divorced from the context of the great (albeit fragmentary) work in which it is contained. In reality, the

---

[5] Ibid.

[6] "We should never doubt that, every time we see people offering texts of the Apostles and Prophets against the Catholic faith, Satan is speaking through them" (ch. 26, p. 99).

[7] Ch. 25, p. 93.

[8] Because public revelation is complete at the death of the last Apostles (DH 3421), heresy is always novel. St. Vincent expresses the proper disposition of every truly Catholic writer upon sacred doctrine when he remarks that his task is "to describe what our ancestors have handed down and entrusted to us . . . more as an honest reporter than as a presumptuous author" (ch. 1, p. 7).

Vincentian Canon is a potent instrument for distinguishing a true from a false development in Christian doctrine.

Various academics and ecclesiastical functionaries are required by the Code of Canon Law[9] and the Code of Canons of the Eastern Churches[10] to recite, upon assuming their offices, the *Professio Fidei* promulgated by John Paul II in 1998.[11] This text consists in the first place of the Niceno-Constantinopolitan Creed[12] and then of three paragraphs intended to encompass the rest of Catholic teaching. They read as follows:

> With firm faith, I also believe everything contained in the word of God, whether written or handed down in Tradition, which the Church, either by a solemn judgment or by the ordinary and universal Magisterium, sets forth to be believed as divinely revealed.
>
> I also firmly accept and hold each and everything definitively proposed by the Church regarding teaching on faith and morals.
>
> Moreover, I adhere with religious submission of will and intellect to the teachings which either the Roman Pontiff or the College of Bishops enunciate when they exercise their authentic Magisterium, even if they do not intend to proclaim these teachings by a definitive act.

The Vincentian Canon is, in fact, a brilliantly succinct instrument for the navigation of the different modes of teaching laid out in the "concluding formula" of the 1998 *Professio Fidei*. There is a distinction in the concluding formula with which Vincent does not deal and that is between the first and second paragraphs. The first paragraph treats of dogmas, that is, truths directly revealed by God, while

---

[9] CIC (1983) § 750.
[10] CCEO (1990) § 598.
[11] John Paul II, *Ad Tuendam Fidem* (1998).
[12] As amended in AD 1014 by the addition of the *filioque* when the Creed of 381 was added to the papal use of the Roman Rite for the Coronation Mass of St. Henry II.

the second paragraph deals with mere doctrines, that is, truths historically or logically connected with revelation but not directly revealed. Both sets of truths are taught infallibly and receive the assent of faith — the former directly (*de fide credenda*) and the latter indirectly (*de fide tenenda*) — in virtue of the direct assent given to the dogma of "the Holy Spirit's assistance to the Magisterium and on the Catholic doctrine of the infallibility of the Magisterium."[13]

The distinctions that concern us here are between the two types of teaching identified in the first paragraph (solemn judgments and the ordinary and universal Magisterium) and the mode of teaching mentioned in the third paragraph, "the teachings which either the Roman Pontiff or the College of Bishops enunciate when they exercise their authentic Magisterium, even if they do not intend to proclaim these teachings by a definitive act."[14] St. Vincent's canon maps very exactly on to these three modes of teaching. "Everywhere" concerns the authentic magisterium, "always" concerns the ordinary and universal magisterium, and "everyone" concerns the solemn judgments of the Church (elsewhere[15] called the "extraordinary magisterium").

The first question, therefore, is "What does the *Catholic* Church teach?" — that is, what is the teaching of that Church which is "everywhere"? Not, in this instance, her *definitive* teaching (we shall come to that) nor yet the more subtle question of the consensus of the Church across all of time, but the normal everyday teaching of the Catholic Church. This is ordinary teaching (not the ordinary and

---

[13] Congregation for the Doctrine of the Faith, *Doctrinal Commentary on the Concluding Formula of the "Professio Fidei,"* no. 6.
[14] The distinction between solemn judgments and the ordinary and universal Magisterium also applies to the sort of teaching described in the second paragraph, "everything definitively proposed by the Church regarding teaching on faith and morals"; but as the distinction between the first and second paragraphs does not concern us here, there is no need to go into that further.
[15] Pius XI, *Mortalium Animos* (1928), §9.

universal magisterium, which is precisely that consensus of the Church across all of time), the kind we mean when we say "What does the Church teach?," "What is in the catechism?," "What did Father say?" It is not infallible but it must enjoy a presumption of reliability if the ordinary teaching organs of the church—the bishops, pastors of parishes, catechisms, etc.—are to function and to have any purpose whatsoever. But it is precisely the ordinary teaching organs of the *Catholic* Church to which we refer, to the authorised teachers of that Church which exists "everywhere," and not some national sect or schismatic movement. This is where the Christian starts when he seeks for a reason for the hope that is in him, in the face of "unlearned and unstable [men who] wrest ... [the] scriptures to their own destruction" (2 Pet 3:16).

But the (merely) authentic magisterium is not infallible, and therefore, if the magisterium is to "guarantee them [the faithful] the objective possibility of professing the true faith without error,"[16] there has to be an answer to the question "What are we to do when the (merely) authentic magisterium fails?" This is when St. Vincent turns to the second element in his canon: "always." Whatever Christ revealed, the Church has *always* believed, and indeed *all* the Church has *always* taught and believed it, in the narrow sense that whenever any authorised preacher in his authentic magisterium teaches anything false, he is acting *ultra vires*.[17] If something,

---

[16] *CCC*, no. 890.

[17] In this sense, therefore, the first test is sufficient—but only if the whole Church is unanimous in the present moment. In that case, the authentic magisterium is visibly identical with the ordinary and universal magisterium. A classic example of this would be the proposition "we must love our enemies," which is unanimously taught in the present by the authentic magisterium and so can be perceived to be taught by the ordinary and universal magisterium. Put differently, the authentic magisterium and the ordinary and universal magisterium are one and the same insofar as any erring exercise of the authentic magisterium is *ultra vires*, but that identity is not detectable unless the exercise of the authentic magisterium is *actually unanimous* in the present. The subject of an act of the authentic magisterium is a given churchman or group

therefore, can be shown ever to have been taught or believed by the whole Church, it must be true, and if anything can be shown to be truly novel (because no one believed it before a certain point), then it must be false. This is because Christ's promise of indefectibility precludes any part of the deposit of faith having disappeared from the Church or having been passed on purely materially such that its meaning was unknown and discovered later only through some new revelation or through the progress of secular knowledge.[18]

This is, however, a negative test. If some purported doctrine is truly novel, then it is false. The fact that the heresy of Simon Magus goes back to apostolic time does not make it true. It is this consideration that draws us on to the third element in Vincent's canon: "What are we to do when the heretics can show evidence of their error being upheld by some even in ancient times?" This difficulty requires us to turn to the solemn judgment of the Church, the extraordinary magisterium, which takes the form of the irreformable decrees of ecumenical councils ("everyone") or the infallible decrees of popes.[19] If such a judgment exists or can be achieved, then the matter is settled and our problem is solved.

---

of churchmen. The subject of the ordinary and universal magisterium is the Church herself.

[18] Cf. DH 3043: Si quis dixerit, fieri posse, ut dogmatibus ab Ecclesia propositis aliquando secundum progressum scientiae sensus tribuendus sit alius ab eo, quem intellexit et intelligit Ecclesia: anathema sit. (If anyone says that it is possible that at some time, given the advancement of knowledge, a sense may be assigned to the dogmas propounded by the church which is different from that which the church has understood and understands: let him be anathema.)

[19] These also constitute an appeal to "everyone" because rejection of such definitions places one outside Catholic communion. Although papal definitons were less common in St. Vincent's time, he does allude to the principle when he mentions the insistence of Pope Celestine that certain heretics should be excluded in advance from doctrinal deliberations. "Rightly we have to bear the responsibility, if by our silence we encourage error. Therefore, those who behave in this way should be rebuked! They should have no right to free speech" (ch. 32, p. 119).

But what if such a judgment does not exist and cannot, for reasons of ecclesiastical or temporal politics, be achieved? How is the faithful Christian to navigate a theological dispute in such circumstances and defend the apostolic faith against heresy? In this case, Vincent explains, he must return to the second element in the canon: "always." On the first occasion, he appealed to antiquity in a general sense. In the second round, he needs to be more discriminating. He must look to Church fathers only in the strict sense: those who have been shown to be authentic teachers of the faith by their sanctity, by their preservation of ecclesiastical communuion, and by their adherence to correct doctrine in all areas in which a judgment of the extraordinary magisterium has already occurred.

Although unanimity in the doctrine of the Church at any time would suffice to demonstrate the truth of a teaching, the appeal is made especially to *antiquity* because the dispersal of the Church increases over time and so the task of demonstrating unanimity without a formally ecumenical decree (or a formal consultation of the dispersed episcopate by the pope) becomes effectively impossible and because the deposit must have been understood correctly by those who first received it or the correct understanding could never have been passed on to all subsequent generations. If the true doctrine of the Church on any point contained in public revelation cannot be established by reason enlightened by faith (not private prophecy) through an examination of the sense in which that revelation was originally understood, then the judgments of the magisterium would be a form of divination or new revelation, and thus, not truly judgments at all.[20]

---

[20] Vincent places into the mouth of the heretic the following striking speech (ch. 21, p. 77): "Come, you poor ignorant people, commonly called Catholics, and learn the true faith which no one knows except ourselves, which was concealed for many centuries, but which lately has been revealed and made manifest. But learn it furtively and secretly; it will delight you. And when you have learned it, teach it covertly, lest

Furthermore, because the objective possibility of professing the true faith without error would not exist between the extinction of the patristic witness on a given point and the issuing of some such blind judgment of infallibility, elements of the deposit would have perished at various points, only to be "topped up" in due course.

The Vincentian Canon is, therefore, really fourfold: everywhere, always (the general witness of antiquity), everyone, and always (the specific witness of the Fathers). It is, accordingly, vital in this fourth stage to be able to distinguish Fathers of the Church in the strict sense from mere ecclesiastical writers such as Tertullian or Origen who might well be witnesses to antiquity in a broad sense but who have fallen into error or heresy on specific points and so must be excluded from the *consensus patrum*.

Living in an era in which the merely authentic papal magisterium is alleged and sometimes frankly admitted to diverge from the merely authentic papal magisterium of former times (and not always far distant times), Vincent's strictures as to how to proceed in such cases are of special relevance. In the Church of God, the teacher's error is the people's temptation, and "the greater the erring teacher, the greater the temptation."[21] We also live in an era in which the mining of ecclesiastical writers (especially Origen) for incautious speculations to support more modern novelties is a cottage industry among academics.[22]

St. Vincent's description of the heretic has a chillingly contemporary ring to it:

---

the world hear it or the Church find out about it. For it is given only to a few to receive the secret of so great a mystery."

[21] Ch. 17, p. 61.

[22] St. Vincent's description of Photinus could be applied to any number of more recent authors (ch. 11, p. 43): "It would take too long to mention all his works, by which he could have been deemed an equal of the most constructive minds in the Church, if he had not, out of impious desire for heretical curiosity, invented some new doctrine or other which infected all his labors with a kind of leprosy and caused his teaching to become more a temptation than an edification in the Church."

They are possessed by a permanent desire to change religion, to add something and to take something away — as though the dogma were not divine, so that it has to be revealed only once. But they take it for a merely human institution, which cannot be perfected except by constant emendations, nay rather, by constant corrections. Yet the divine prophecies say: "Pass not beyond the ancient bounds which thy fathers have set" (Prov. 22:28).[23]

In our times, St. Vincent's clear distinctions on this point take on exceptional importance. The fact that they come down to us from the patristic age itself makes them particularly powerful. The ancient boundaries of the Fathers need ready and valliant defenders as never before; and if the inspired word of God will perforce be the two edged sword in their hands, they will have Vincent's song upon their lips. As the First Vatican Council resoundingly proclaimed:

May understanding, knowledge, and wisdom increase as ages and centuries roll along, and greatly and vigorously flourish, in each and all, in the individual and the whole Church: but this, only in its own proper kind, that is to say, in the same doctrine, the same sense, and the same understanding.

---

[23] Ch. 21, p. 75.

SANCTORVM
PRESBYTERORVM
SALVIANI
MASSILIENSIS
ET
VINCENTII
LIRINENSIS
OPERA.

STEPHANVS BALVZIVS Tutelensis
ad fidem veterum codicum MSS. emendavit,
Notisque illustravit.

EDITIO SECVNDA.

PARISIIS,

Apud Franciscum Muguet Regis
& illustrissimi Archiepiscopi Parisiensis
Typographum.
MDCLXIX.

COMMONITORIUM

pro

Catholicae Fidei
Antiquitate et
Universitate,

ADVERSUS PROFANAS OMNIUM
HAERETICORUM NOVITATES

VINCENTIUS
LIRINENSIS

COMMONITORY
for
THE ANTIQUITY AND UNIVERSALITY OF THE CATHOLIC FAITH,
AGAINST THE PROFANE NOVELTIES OF ALL HERETICS[†]

VINCENT
OF LÉRINS

[†] This is the title of the work in the first edition of Sichardus (Basel, 1528): "In defense of the antiquity and universality of the Catholic faith, [the work] of Vincent of Lérins against the profane innovations of all heretics." Gennadius states (*De vir. ill.* 64) that the title should be "Of the Pilgrim, against heretics." Also, in the codices at the end of the work we read: "The explanation of the treatise of the Pilgrim against heretics." In the Paris codices, the work is simply called "The Commonitories."

Dicente Scriptura et monente, *Interroga patres tuos, et dicent tibi; seniores tuos, et adnuntiabunt tibi*, et item, *Verbis sapientium adcommoda aurem tuam*, et item, *Fili mi, hos sermones ne obliviscaris, mea autem verba custodiat cor tuum*, videtur mihi minimo omnium servorum Dei Peregrino quod res non minimae utilitatis, Domino adjuvante, futura sit, si ea quae fideliter a sanctis patribus accepi litteris comprehendam, infirmitati certe propriae pernecessaria, quippe cum adsit in promptu unde imbecillitas memoriae meae adsidua lectione reparetur.

Ad quod me negotium non solum fructus operis, sed etiam consideratio temporis et opportunitas loci adhortatur.

Tempus: propterea quod cum ab eo omnia humana rapiantur, et nos ex eo aliquid invicem rapere debemus quod in vitam proficiat aeternam; praesertim cum et appropinquantis divini Judicii terribilis quaedam exspectatio augeri efflagitet studia Religionis, et novorum Haereticorum fraudulentia multum curae et attentionis indicat.

Locus autem, quod urbium frequentiam turbasque vitantes, remotioris villulae et in ea secretum monasterii incolamus habitaculum, ubi absque magna distractione fieri possit illud quod canitur in psalmo: *Vacate, inquit, et videte quoniam ego sum Dominus*. Sed et propositi nostri ratio in id convenit; quippe qui cum aliquandiu variis ac tristibus saecularis militiae turbinibus volveremur, tandem nos in portum Religionis, cunctis semper fidissimum, Christo adspirante condidimus;

1

HOLY SCRIPTURE ADMONISHES US: "ASK thy fathers, and they will declare to thee: thy elders and they will tell thee" (Deut. 32:7); and again: "Incline thy ear and hear the words of the wise" (Prov. 22:17); and again: "My son, forget not my law: and let thy heart keep my commandments" (Prov. 3:1). According to these words, it seems to me, Peregrinus,[1] the least of all the servants of God, that it will be rather useful for me to write down, with the help of the Lord, what I have faithfully received from the holy fathers.[2] Of this I shall certainly be in great need in my infirmity, for my memory may be refreshed by persistent reading if I have these matters down in writing.

I am induced to perform this task not only for the results of the work but also because I have the time and a suitable place to do it.

As for the time: since time snatches away all things human, we ought to snatch from it something which may profit us unto life eternal. We are moved particularly by the terrible fear of the approaching Judgment which urges us to increase our studies of religion, and by the deceitfulness of the new heretics which requires much careful attention.

As for the place: far from the masses that overcrowd large cities, I am living in a very remote spot where, within the cell of a monastery with nothing to distract me, I can practice what is sung in the psalm: "Be still and see that I am God" (Ps. 45:11). This way of life is well suited to the work I am planning to do. Long involved in various unstable and saddening whirlpools of secular strife, I finally arrived, under Christ's inspiration, at the harbor of religion, always the safest place for everyone. There,

---

[1] We read in Gennadius that Vincent adopted this name.
[2] But to this statement the *Commonitories* themselves, so far as they are extant, give only little support, for in them does not appear the collected testimony of the Fathers, but certain notes and rules whereby Catholic doctrine may be distinguished from heresy.

ut ibi depositis vanitatis ac superbiae flatibus, Christianae humilitatis sacrificio placantes Deum, non solum praesentis vitae naufragia, sed etiam futuri saeculi incendia vitare possimus.

Sed jam in nomine Domini quod instat adgrediar, ut scilicet a majoribus tradita et apud nos deposita describam, relatoris fide potius quam auctoris praesumptione; hac tamen scribendi lege servata, ut nequaquam omnia, sed tantum necessaria quaeque perstringam, neque id ornato et exacto sed facili communique sermone, ut pleraque significata potius quam explicata videantur. Scribant ii laute et accurate qui ad hoc munus vel ingenii fiducia vel officii ratione ducuntur. Me vero sublevandae recordationis vel potius oblivionis meae gratia Commonitorium mihimet parasse suffecerit: quod tamen paulatim, recolendo quae didici, emendare et implere quotidie, Domino praestante, conabor. Atque hoc ipsum idcirco praemonui, ut si forte elapsum nobis, in manus sanctorum devenerit, nihil in eo temere reprehendant, quod adhuc videant promissa emendatione limandum.

II

S AEPE IGITUR MAGNO STUDIO et summa attentione perquirens a quamplurimis sanctitate et doctrina praestantibus viris quonam modo possim certa quadam et quasi generali ac regulari via catholicae fidei veritatem ab haereticae pravitatis falsitate discernere, hujusmodi semper responsum ab omnibus fere rettuli, quod sive ego, sive quis alius vellet exsurgentium haereticorum fraudes deprehendere laqueosque vitare, et in fide sana sanus atque integer permanere, duplici modo munire fidem

after the storms of vanity and pride have ceased, I may propitiate God by the sacrifice of Christian humility and thus avoid not only the shipwrecks of the present life, but also the flames of the world to come.

But now it is time for me to begin, in the name of the Lord, my work, namely, to describe what our ancestors have handed down and entrusted to us. I shall do this more as an honest reporter than as a presumptuous author. I shall follow this plan in my writing. I shall not cover everything, but only the essential points; not in an embellished and meticulous form, but in easy and popular language. In this way most of the points will appear to be indicated rather than developed. Let those make use of a flowery and precise style who approach such a task either from confidence in their own ability or through a sense of duty. As for me, I shall be satisfied to compose this *Commonitory* for my own use, to aid my memory, or, rather, [to check] my forgetfulness. In any case, with the Lord's help, I shall do my best recalling step by step what I have learned, emending and filling out my knowledge from day to day. I have prefaced my work with this warning so that in case it slips from my hands into those of saintly persons,[3] they may not hastily censure certain passages, but remember that I have promised to correct and improve them.

2

WITH GREAT ZEAL AND FULL ATTENtion I often inquired from many men, outstanding in sanctity and doctrinal knowledge, how, in a concise and, so to speak, general and ordinary way, I might be able to discern the truth of the Catholic faith from the falsity of heretical corruption. From almost all of them I always received the answer that if I or someone else wanted to expose the frauds of the heretics and to escape their snares and to remain sound in the integrity of faith, I had, with

---

[3] Of those who have forsaken the world, i.e., priests and monks.

suam, Domino adjuvante, deberet: primum scilicet divinae legis auctoritate, tum deinde Ecclesiae catholicae traditione.

Hic forsitan requirat aliquis: Cum sit perfectus Scripturarum Canon, sibique ad omnia
satis superque sufficiat, quid opus est ut ei Ecclesiasticae intelligentiae jungatur auctoritas?

Quia videlicet Scripturam sacram pro ipsa
sua altitudine non uno eodemque sensu universi
accipiunt, sed ejusdem eloquia aliter atque aliter
alius atque alius interpretatur; ut paene quot
homines sunt, tot illinc sententiae erui posse
videantur. Aliter namque illam Novatianus, aliter
Sabellius, aliter Donatus exponit, aliter Arius,
Eunomius, Macedonius; aliter Photinus, Apollinaris, Priscillianus, aliter Jovinianus, Pelagius,
Caelestius; aliter postremo Nestorius. Atque
idcirco multum necesse est, propter tantos tam
varii erroris anfractus, ut propheticae et apostolicae interpretationis linea secundum Ecclesiastici
et Catholici sensus normam dirigatur.

In ipsa item Catholica Ecclesia magnopere
curandum est ut id teneamus quod ubique, quod
semper, quod ab omnibus creditum est. Hoc est
etenim vere proprieque catholicum, quod ipsa vis

the help of the Lord, to fortify that faith in a twofold manner: first, by the authority[4] of the divine Law; second, by the tradition of the Catholic Church.

Here, perhaps, someone may ask: Since the canon of Scripture is complete and more than sufficient in itself, why is it necessary to add to it the authority of ecclesiastical interpretation?

As a matter of fact, [we must answer,] Holy Scripture, because of its depth, is not universally accepted in one and the same sense. The same text is interpreted differently by different people, so that one may almost gain the impression that it can yield as many different meanings as there are men. Novatianus, for example, expounds a passage in one way; Sabellius, in another; Donatus,[5] in another. Arius, and Eunomius and Macedonius read it differently; so do Photinus,[6] Apollinaris, and Priscillianus; in another way, Jovinianus, Pelagius, and Celestius; finally, in still another, Nestorius. Thus, because of the great distortions caused by various errors, it is, indeed, necessary that the trend of the interpretation of the prophetic and apostolic writings be directed in accordance with the rule of the ecclesiastical and Catholic meaning.

In the Catholic Church itself, every care should be taken to hold fast to what has been believed everywhere, always, and by all. This is truly and properly "Catholic,"[7]

---

[4] See the interesting comment of Tertullian, *De praescr.* 16–19 (Rauschen, 11).

[5] We must understand this to refer to that Donatus who was Bishop of Casae Nigrae in Numidia, "who, coming from Numidia, and drawing to himself the bishops of his own faction against Caecilian, creating division, among the Christian people, ordained Majorinus bishop in Carthage," or Donatus the Great, who succeeded Majorinus to the See of Carthage, "who by his eloquence so strengthened this heresy that many thought that because of him they should rather be called Donatists" (Augustine, *De haeresibus* 69).

[6] This Bishop of Sirmium (chief city of Lower Pannonia, now Mitrovica, Kosovo), who preached that Christ was merely a man endowed with divine virtues and adopted by God, was removed from his See by the Synod of Sirmium in 351 and died in exile in 376.

[7] The fold of Christ is first called the Catholic Church (*katholikè ekklesía*) by St. Ignatius, *Ep. ad Smyrn.* 8. A certain explanation of the name is given

nominis ratioque declarat, quae omnia fere universaliter comprehendit. Sed hoc ita demum fiet,
si sequamur universitatem, antiquitatem, consensionem. Sequemur autem universitatem hoc
modo, si hanc unam fidem veram esse fateamur
quam tota per orbem terrarum confitetur Ecclesia; antiquitatem vero ita, si ab his sensibus nul-
latenus recedamus quos sanctos majores ac patres
nostros celebrasse manifestum est: consensionem
quoque itidem, si, in ipsa vetustate, omnium vel
certe paene omnium sacerdotum pariter et magistrorum definitiones sententiasque sectemur.

III

QUID IGITUR TUNC FACIET
Christianus catholicus, si se aliqua Ecclesiae particula ab universalis fidei communione
praeciderit? Quid utique nisi ut pestifero cor-
ruptoque membro sanitatem universi corporis
anteponat? Quid si novella aliqua contagio non
jam portiunculam tantum, sed totam pariter
Ecclesiam commaculare conetur? Tunc item
providebit ut antiquitati inhaereat, quae pror-
sum jam non potest ab ulla novitatis fraude
seduci. Quid si in ipsa vetustate, duorum aut
trium hominum, vel certe civitatis unius aut
etiam provinciae alicujus error deprehendatur?
Tunc omnino curabit ut paucorum temeritati vel
inscitiae, si qua sunt, universaliter antiquitus universalis Concilii decreta praeponat. Quid si tale
aliquid emergat ubi nihil hujusmodi reperiatur?
Tunc operam dabit ut collatas inter se majorum
consulat interrogetque sententias, eorum dumtaxat qui diversis licet temporibus et locis, in

as indicated by the force and etymology of the name itself,
which comprises everything truly universal. This general
rule will be truly applied if we follow the principles of
universality, antiquity, and consent. We do so in regard
to universality if we confess that faith alone to be true
which the entire Church confesses all over the world. [We
do so] in regard to antiquity if we in no way deviate from
those interpretations which our ancestors and fathers[8]
have manifestly proclaimed as inviolable. [We do so] in
regard to consent if, in this very antiquity, we adopt the
definitions and propositions of all, or almost all, the bishops[9] and doctors.

3

WHAT, THEREFORE, WILL THE CATH-
olic Christian do if some members of the Church
have broken away from the communion of universal faith?
What else, but prefer the sanity of the body universal to the
pestilence of the corrupt member? What if a new contagion
strives to infect not only a small part but the whole of the
Church? Then, he will endeavor to adhere to the antiquity
which is evidently beyond the danger of being seduced by
the deceit of some novelty. What if in antiquity itself an
error is detected, on the part of two or three men, or even
on the part of a city or a province? Then, he will take care
to prefer the decrees of a previous ecumenical council (if
there was one) to the temerity and ignorance of a small
group. Finally, what if such an error arises and nothing like
a council can be found? Then, he will take pains to consult
and interrogate the opinions of his predecessors, compar-
ing them with [one another only as regards the opinions

---

by St. Optatus, *De schism. Donat.* 2.1: "The proper significance of the name
Catholic will be had when that is called Catholic which is in accordance
with reason (*catholicus — katà lógon*? du Pin) and diffused everywhere."
The accepted etymology is καθόλου, "according to the whole," which is
formed of κατά (*kata*) and ὅλος (*holos*); in other words, universal.

[8] See ch. 28 and ch. 29.
[9] The text has *sacerdotum* (priests).

unius tamen Ecclesiae Catholicae communione
et fide permanentes, magistri probabiles exstiterunt; et quicquid non unus aut duo tantum, sed
omnes pariter uno eodemque consensu aperte,
frequenter, perseveranter tenuisse, scripsisse,
docuisse cognoverit, id sibi quoque intelligat
absque ulla dubitatione credendum.

IV

S ED UT PLANIORA FIANT QUAE
dicimus, exemplis singillatim illustranda
sunt et paulo uberius exaggeranda; ne immo-
dicae brevitatis studio rapiantur rerum pondera
orationis celeritate.

Tempore Donati, a quo Donatistae, cum sese
multa pars Africae in erroris sui furias praecipita-
ret, cumque immemor nominis, religionis, pro-
fessionis, unius hominis sacrilegam temeritatem
Ecclesiae Christi praeponeret, tunc quicumque
per Africam constituti, profano schismate dete-
stato, universis mundi Ecclesiis adsociati sunt,
soli ex illis omnibus intra sacraria catholicae fidei
salvi esse potuerunt; egregiam profecto relin-
quentes posteris formam, quemadmodum scilicet deinceps, bono more, unius aut certe paucorum vesaniae universorum sanitas anteferretur.

Item quando Arianorum venenum non jam
portiunculam quamdam, sed paene orbem
totum contaminaverat, adeo ut prope cunctis
Latini sermonis Episcopis partim vi, partim
fraude deceptis, caligo quaedam mentibus offun-
deretur, quidnam potissimum in tanta rerum

of] those who, though they lived in various periods and at different periods and at different places, nevertheless remained in the communion and faith of the one Catholic Church, and who therefore have become reliable authorities. As he will discover, he must also believe without hesitation whatever not only one or two but all equally and with one and the same consent, openly, frequently, and persistently have held, written, and taught.

4

TO MAKE CLEARER WHAT WE SAY, examples will be given for each instance, and we must dwell on them more extensively. For it must not be that our eagerness to be brief deprives the matters in question of their weight by an overhasty presentation.

In the time of Donatus (from whom rose the Donatists), a great part of Africa rushed[10] into the madness of his error and, forgetful of name, religion, and profession, preferred the sacrilegious rashness of a single man to the Church of Christ. Then, of all the people of Africa, only those who detested this profane schism and remained associated with the universal Church were able to keep themselves safe within the sanctuary of Catholic faith. Thus, they left an outstanding example to posterity of the way in which the soundness of the body universal ought rightly to be set above the unsoundness of a single man or even of a few individuals.

Similarly, when the poison of Arianism had infected not only a small part but nearly the entire world[11]—to such an extent that most bishops of the Latin tongue were led into error, partly by force and partly by fraud, and a kind of darkness had obscured their minds, depriving them of insight into what it was best to do in such a confused

---

[10] See Possidius, *Vita S. Augustini* 7.
[11] Jerome (*Dial. adv. Luciferianos* 19) complains thus of the Synod of Rimini, held in 359: "The whole world groaned, and was amazed to find itself Arian."

confusione sequendum foret, tunc quisquis verus
Christi amator et cultor exstitit, antiquam fidem
novellae perfidiae praeferendo, nulla contagii
ipsius peste maculatus est. Cujus quidem temporis periculo satis superque monstratum est
quantum invehatur calamitatis novelli dogmatis
inductione. Hunc siquidem non solum parvae
res, sed etiam maximae labefactatae sunt. Nec
enim tantum adfinitates, cognationes, amicitiae,
domus, verum etiam urbes, populi, provinciae,
nationes, universum postremo Romanum Imperium funditus concussum et emotum est. Namque cum prophana ipsa Arianorum novitas, velut
quaedam Bellona aut furia, capto primo omnium
Imperatore, cuncta deinde palatii culmina legi-
bus novis subjugasset, nequaquam deinceps
destitit universa miscere atque vexare, privata ac
publica, sacra prophanaque omnia, nullum boni
et veri gerere discrimen, sed quoscumque conli-
buisset, tamquam de loco superiore percutere.

Tunc temeratae conjuges, depullatae viduae,
prophanatae virgines, monasteria demolita,
disturbati clerici, verberati levitae, acti in exi-
lium sacerdotes, oppleta sanctis ergastula, car-
ceres, metalla: quorum pars maxima, interdictis
urbibus, protrusi atque extorres, inter deserta,
speluncas, feras, saxa, nuditate, fame, siti affecti,
contriti et tabefacti sunt. Atque haec omnia
numquid ullam aliam ob causam, nisi utique
dum pro caelesti dogmate humanae superstitio-
nes introducuntur, dum bene fundata antiquitas
scelesta novitate subruitur, dum superiorum
instituta violantur, dum rescinduntur scita
patrum, dum convelluntur definita majorum,
dum sese intra sacratae atque incorruptae vetustatis castissimos limites prophanae ac novellae
curiositatis libido non continet?

situation — then each true lover and worshiper of Christ preferred the ancient faith to the modern falsehood, and thus remained untouched by the infection of that plague. The disaster of that perilous period demonstrates abundantly what calamity is brought about by the induction of a novel dogma. Not only were matters of small moment destroyed, but also those of the greatest import were affected.[12] Not only personal relations, kinship, friendships, homes, but even cities, peoples, provinces, nations, finally, the whole Roman Empire were rocked and shaken to their foundations. When this profane Arian novelty, like Bellona[13] or a Fury, had first of all captured the emperor[14] and then subjugated to the new laws the leaders in the imperial palace as well, it no longer avoided mixing up and disturbing everything, public and private interests, sacred and profane. It did not discriminate in favor of the good and the true; it struck down whomever it capriciously selected, as though it were superior to them.

Then wives were dishonored, widows desecrated, virgins ravished, monasteries demolished, clerics thrown into panic, Levites beaten, priests exiled. Prisons, jails, and mines were overcrowded with saintly persons. Most of them, forbidden to enter the cities, hunted and exiled, exposed to life in deserts, caves, among wild beasts and amid rocks, exhausted by exposure, hunger, and thirst, perished. And all this for no other reason than that human superstitions were substituted for divine dogma; that well-founded tradition was ruined by criminal novelties; that institutions established by authority were violated; that the wisdom of the fathers was rescinded; that the teaching of the elders was thrown into confusion; that the lust for profane and novel curiosity did not contain itself within the most unpolluted bounds of a sacred and uncorrupted antiquity.

---

[12] The allusion is to Sallust, *Jug.* 10.

[13] Bellona was a goddess of the Sabines, the companion or wife of Mars.

[14] Constantius.

V

SED FORSITAN ODIO NOVITATIS et amore vetustatis haec fingimus. Quisquis hoc aestimat, beato saltem credat Ambrosio, qui, in secundo ad Imperatorem Gratianum libro, acerbitatem temporis ipse deplorans, ait: *Sed jam satis,* inquit, *omnipotens Deus, nostro exilio nostroque sanguine Confessorum neces, exilia Sacerdotum, et nefas tantae impietatis eluimus. Satis claruit eos qui violaverint fidem tutos esse non posse.* Item in tertio ejusdem operis libro: *Servemus igitur,* inquit, *praecepta majorum, nec haereditaria signacula ausi rudis temeritate violemus. Librum signatum illum propheticum non Seniores, non Potestates, non Angeli, non Archangeli aperire ausi sunt: soli Christo explanandi ejus praerogativa servata est. Librum sacerdotalem quis nostrum resignare audeat, signatum a Confessoribus, et multorum jam martyrio consecratum? Quem qui resignare coacti sunt postea tamen damnata fraude signarunt; qui violare non ausi sunt, Confessores et martyres exstiterunt. Quomodo fidem eorum possumus denegare quorum victoriam praedicamus?*

5

OR IS IT THAT WE FANCY ALL THIS, because of our hatred of novelty and our love of what was established of old? Whoever harbors this suspicion should at least give ear to blessed Ambrose, who, in the second book of his work dedicated to Emperor Gratian, in which he deplores the rudeness of his age, has this to say: "But by now, Almighty God, we have through our ruin and our blood sufficiently expiated the murder of confessors, the exile of priests, and the wickedness of such atrocious impiety. It is now sufficiently evident that those who violated the faith cannot live in security."[15] And he says, in the third book of that same work: "Let us preserve the precepts of our ancestors and not violate the stamp of tradition in a mood of reckless and daring boldness. That sealed prophetic book neither the elders nor the powers nor the angels nor the archangels have dared to open; to Christ alone is reserved the prerogative of explaining it.[16] Who among us would dare to unseal the sacerdotal book confirmed by the confessors[17] and now consecrated by the martyrdom of so many? Those who were forced to subscribe to it retracted this later on, after the fraud was denounced;[18] those who did not dare to violate it became confessors and martyrs. How, then, can we deny the faith of those whose victory we proclaim?"[19]

---

[15] *De fide* 2.6.141.

[16] Rev. 5:1ff.

[17] In the third and fourth centuries, those were called Confessors who confessed the Name of Christ before a Judge, or in chains and prison (cf. Cyprian, *Ep.* 37.1). Later, all those who lived in and died for Christ were accorded the title and honor of Confessor.

[18] Ambrose is speaking of the bishops, worn down by poverty and old age, whom Constantius, in 359, in the Synod of Rimini, compelled to abjure the faith, by denying them permission to return. When the Emperor died a short time later, almost all condemned the subscription and the Arian heresy, especially the bishops of Gaul under the leadership of St. Hilary, in the Synod of Paris, 361 (see Jerome, *Dial. adv. Luciferianos* 19).

[19] *De fide* 3.15.128.

Praedicamus plane, inquam, oh, venerande Ambrosi! Praedicamus plane, laudantesque miramur. Nam quis ille tam demens est qui eos, etsi adsequi non evaleat, non exoptet sequi quos a defensione fidei majorum nulla vis depulit, non minae, non blandimenta, non vita, non mors, non palatium, non satellites, non Imperator, non imperium, non homines, non daemones? quos, inquam, pro religiosae vetustatis tenacitate tanto munere Dominus dignos judicavit ut per eos prostratas restauraret Ecclesias, exstinctos spiritales populos vivificaret, dejectas sacerdotum coronas, reponeret, nefarias illas novellae impietatis non litteras, sed lituras, infuso caelitus Episcopis fidelium lacrimarum fonte, deleret, universum postremo jam paene mundum saeva repentinae haereseos tempestate perculsum ad antiquam fidem a novella perfidia, ad antiquam sanitatem a novitatis vesania, ad antiquam lucem a novitatis caecitate revocaret.

Sed in hac divina quadam Confessorum virtute illud est etiam nobis vel maxime considerandum, quod tunc apud ipsam Ecclesiae vetustatem non partis alicujus, sed universitatis ab iis est suscepta defensio. Neque enim fas erat, ut tanti ac tales viri unius aut duorum hominum errabundas sibique ipsis contrarias suspiciones tam magno molimine adsererent, aut vero pro alicujus provinciolae temeraria quadam conspiratione certarent, sed omnium sanctae Ecclesiae sacerdotum apostolicae et catholicae veritatis haeredum decreta et definita sectantes, maluerunt semetipsos quam vetustae universitatis fidem prodere. Unde et ad tantam gloriam pervenire meruerunt, ut non solum Confessores, verum etiam Confessorum principes jure meritoque habeantur.

We proclaim it, indeed, venerable Ambrose; we give them praise and admiration. For who is so foolish as not to desire (although he may not be able to reach such heights) to follow those whom no force could keep from defending the faith of their ancestors — no threats, no blandishments, neither life nor death, not the palace, not the courtiers, not the emperor, not the empire, not men, not demons? These, I say, because of their tenacious attachment to the ancient faith, were deemed worthy by the Lord of so great a reward that through them He restored battered churches, brought to life peoples that were spiritually dead, and restored the stolen crowns of priests. He erased those nefarious, not letters but blots, of the new impiety with the tears shed by the faithful bishops, a fountain divinely fed. Finally, He recalled the world, which had been almost completely shaken by the furious hurricane of unexpected heresy, from the new perfidy to the old faith, from modern unreasonableness to ancient sanity, from the blindness of novelty to the ancient light.

What we have to consider above all, when admiring the quasi-divine power of the confessors, is that they took up the defense of the old tradition of the Church, not with regard to a particular group, but with regard to a whole body. Indeed, it would not have been possible for such outstanding men to assert, with such elaborate equipment, the erroneous and self-contradictory assumptions of one or two individuals, or to fight for the cause of some impudent conspiracy that might arise in some corner of a province. No, what they actually did was to stay in line with the decrees and definitions[20] of all the priests of Holy Church as the heirs of Apostolic and Catholic Truth. They preferred to surrender themselves rather than the faith universally held from the beginning. For this reason, they deserved to rise to such a height of glory that they rightly and deservedly are regarded not as mere confessors, but rather as princes among confessors.

---

[20] Especially the decrees of the Nicene Council.

VI

MAGNUM HOC IGITUR EORUM-
dem beatorum exemplum, planeque
divinum, et veris quibusque Catholicis inde-
fessa meditatione recolendum, qui modum
septemplicis candelabri septena sancti Spiritus
luce radiante, clarissimam posteris formulam
praemonstrarunt quonam modo deinceps per
singula quaeque errorum vaniloquia, sacratae
vetustatis auctoritate prophanae novitatis con-
teratur audacia. Neque hoc sane novum. Siquidem mos iste semper in Ecclesia viguit ut quo
quisque foret religiosor, eo promptius novellis
adintentionibus contrairet.

Exemplis talibus plena sunt omnia. Sed ne
longum fiat, unum aliquod, et hoc ab Apostolica potissimum Sede sumemus; ut omnes luce
clarius videant beatorum Apostolorum beata
successio quanta vi semper, quanto studio,
quanta contentione defenderit susceptae semel
Religionis integritatem. Quondam igitur vene-
rabilis memoriae Agrippinus Carthaginensis
Episcopus, primus omnium mortalium contra
divinum Canonem, contra universalis Ecclesiae
regulam, contra sensum omnium consacerdo-
tum, contra morem atque instituta majorum,
rebaptizandum esse censebat. Quae praesump-
tio tantum mali invexit, ut non solum Haereticis omnibus formam sacrilegii, sed etiam
quibusdam Catholicis occasionem praebuerit
erroris. Cum ergo undique ad novitatem rei

6

A GREAT AND EVIDENTLY DIVINE EXAM-
ple that should be meditated upon and recalled again
and again by every true Catholic is given by those blessed
persons who, like the seven-branched candlestick radiat-
ing the sevenfold light of the Holy Spirit, manifested to
posterity the clearest formula for the way in which the
rashness of profane novelty, with all its boastful display
of errors, is to be crushed from now on by the authority
of sacred tradition. This method, to be sure, is not at all
new. It has been an established custom in the Church
that the more devout a person is, the more prompt he is
to oppose innovations.

History offers a wealth of such examples. But, in
order to be brief, we take only one, but one of exceptional weight—namely, from the Apostolic See[21]—so
that it may appear clearer than daylight to all with what
vigor, zeal, and fighting spirit the blessed successors of
the blessed Apostles have defended the integrity of the
religion that they had accepted once and for all. This is
what happened. Bishop Agrippinus of Carthage,[22] of venerable memory, was the first to hold that rebaptism might
be permitted—contrary to divine Law;[23] contrary to the
rule of the Church Universal, contrary to the opinion
of all of his fellow bishops, contrary to the customs and
institutions of our forefathers. This false doctrine carried
with it so much evil that it afforded not only all heretics a pattern for sacrilege, but also some Catholics an
opportunity for error.[24] When, then, people everywhere

---

[21] The Roman See (cf. Tertullian, *De praescr.* 20).

[22] Agrippinus, in a council of Africans and Numidians at Carthage,
about 220, decreed that baptisms of heretics were invalid. See Cyprian,
Ep. 71.4 and 73.3. The bishops of Asia, in the Synods of Iconium and
Synnada (about 230), gave the same decision, as Dionysius, Bishop of
Alexandria (cf. Eusebius, *Historia ecclesiastica* 7.7) and Bishop Firmilianus
(Cyprian, *Ep.* 75.7) bear witness.

[23] That is, contrary to Sacred Scripture.

[24] The custom of rebaptizing heretics flourished.

cuncti reclamarent, atque omnes quaquaversum
sacerdotes pro suo quisque studio retinerentur,
tunc beatae memoriae Papa Stephanus apostolicae Sedis antistes, cum ceteris quidem collegis
suis, sed tamen prae ceteris restitit, dignum, ut
opinor, existimans si reliquos omnes tantum
fidei devotione vinceret quantum loci auctoritate superabat. Denique in Epistola quae tunc
ad Africam missa est, his verbis sanxit: *Nihil
novandum nisi quod traditum est.* Intelligebat
etenim vir sanctus et prudens nihil aliud rationem pietatis admittere, nisi ut omnia, qua fide
a patribus suscepta forent, eadem fide filiis
consignarentur; nosque Religionem, non qua
vellemus ducere, sed potius qua illa duceret
sequi oportere; idque esse proprium Christianae modestiae et gravitatis, non sua posteris
tradere, sed a majoribus accepta servare. Quis
ergo tunc universi negotii exitus? Quis utique
nisi usitatus et solitus? Retenta est scilicet antiquitas, explosa novitas.

Sed forte tunc ipsi novitiae adinventioni
patrocinia defuerunt? Immo vero tanta vis
ingenii adfuit, tanta eloquentiae flumina, tantus adsertorum numerus, tanta verisimilitudo,
tanta divinae legis oracula, sed plane novo ac
malo more intellecta, ut mihi omnis illa con-
spiratio nullo modo destrui potuisse videatur
nisi sola tanti moliminis causa ipsa illa suscepta,
ipsa defensa, laudata novitatis professio destitu-
isset. Quid postremo? Ipsius Africani Concilii
sive decreti quae vires? Donante Deo, nullae;
sed universa tamquam somnia, tamquam fabu-
lae, tamquam superflua, abolita, antiquata cal-
cata sunt.

protested against this novelty and priests from all corners of the world—each according to the degree of his
zeal—strove against it, Pope Stephen, of blessed memory,
who then held the Apostolic See, opposed it, together with
his colleagues, yet more earnestly than they. He apparently
considered it fitting to surpass all others in his devotion to
the faith, inasmuch as he was superior to them by virtue
of his office.[25] In an epistle, which he thereupon sent to
Africa, he stated it as a rule that "nothing new is to be
accepted; only what has been handed down by tradition
[should be]." For that saintly and prudent man realized
that the principle of piety admits of only one attitude:
namely, that everything be transferred to the sons in the
same spirit of faith in which it was accepted by the fathers;
that religion should not lead us whither we want to go, but
that we must follow whither it leads; and that it is proper
to Christian modesty and earnestness not to transfer to
posterity one's own ideas, but to preserve those received
from one's ancestors. To resume: What was the final issue
of the whole problem? What else, but the rule to which
we are used and accustomed? Antiquity was retained;
novelty, repulsed.

But, perhaps only the necessary patronage was lacking for establishing the innovation? Quite the contrary.
They had at their disposal such strength of ingenuity, such
streams of eloquence, such numerous followers, so great a
resemblance to the true, so many references to the divine
Law (obviously interpreted, however, in a new and wrong
sense) that—as it seems to me—the whole conspiracy
could not have been crushed if it had not been overthrown
by reason of terrific weight, namely, by the proclamation
on its *novelty*, which has been accepted, defended, and so
highly praised. What was the final impact of this African
council[26] and its decrees? Thanks be to God, there was

---

[25] *Loci auctoritate*, i.e., through the authority of his See.
[26] Three Councils on the rebaptism of heretics were held at Carthage,
St. Cyprian presiding: the first in 255, the second in 256, the third on

Et, o rerum mira conversio! Auctores ejusdem opinionis Catholici, consectatores vero Haeretici judicantur; absolvuntur magistri, condemnantur discipuli; conscriptores librorum filii regni erunt, adsertores vero gehenna suscipiet. Nam quis ille tam demens est qui illud sanctorum omnium et Episcoporum et Martyrum lumen beatissimum Cyprianum cum ceteris collegis suis in aeternum dubitet regnaturum esse cum Christo? Aut quis tam contra sacrilegus qui Donatistas et ceteras pestes, quae illius auctoritate Concilii rebaptizare se jactitant, in sempiternum neget arsuros esse cum diabolo?

VII

QUOD QUIDEM MIHI DIVINITUS videtur promulgatum esse judicium propter eorum maxime fraudulentiam qui cum sub alieno nomine haeresim concinnare machinentur, captant plerumque veteris cujuspiam viri scripta paulo involutius edita, quae pro ipsa sui obscuritate dogmati suo quasi congruant; ut illud nescio quid quodcunque proferunt, neque primi neque soli sentire videantur. Quorum ego nequitiam duplici odio dignam judico, vel eo quod haereseos

none. The whole matter was abolished, rejected, and trodden upon[27]—like a dream, like a fable, like an empty thing.

And now, what an amazing reversal of the situation! The authors of that same opinion are adjudged to be Catholics, but the followers, heretics;[28] the masters are absolved, the disciples, condemned; the writers of the books will be children in the Kingdom, the adherents of their doctrine will be in Gehenna. For who would be so foolish as to doubt that the most blessed Cyprian, the light of all saints and bishops and martyrs, will with his other colleagues reign with Christ in eternity? Or who, on the other hand, would be so sacrilegious as to deny that the Donatists and the rest of the pests who pride themselves in rebaptism, under the authority of that council, will burn forever with the Devil?

7

I N MY OPINION, THIS JUDGMENT [OF THE Church on rebaptism, as discussed in the preceding chapter] has been promulgated by divine wisdom. Especially is this so because of the fraudulence of those men who try to make it seem that their heresy is something that has a different name; who often seize upon some of the more involved writings of an ancient author, which, merely because of their obscurity, seem to stand in agreement with the new dogma these men propose. By these means, what they profess will not make them appear as though they were the first and only ones to have sensed it. In my judgment,

---

September 1, 256. Vincentius mentions here the third, in which the eighty-seven bishops who were present agreed with Cyprian.

[27] The decree of that third African council was set aside both by the agreement of the entire Catholic Church and by the eighth canon of the Council of Arles, held in 314. Jerome (*Dial. ad Luciferianos* 23) also states: "At last these very bishops who had agreed with him [Cyprian] as to the rebaptism of heretics, when they returned to the ancient custom, issued a new decree." But the testimony is not trustworthy.

[28] That is, the authors of rebaptism, as St. Cyprian remained in communion with those who did not assent to it (see Augustine, *De bapt.* 3.2), but those who later embraced their opinion were adjudged heretics.

venenum propinare aliis non pertimescunt, vel eo
etiam quod sancti cujusque viri memoriam tamquam sopitos jam cineres prophana manu venti-
lant, et quae silentio sepeliri oportebat, rediviva
opinione diffamant, sequentes omnino vestigia
auctoris sui Cham, qui nuditatem venerandi Noe
non modo operire neglexit, verum quoque irri-
dendam ceteris enuntiavit. Unde tantam laesae
pietatis meruit offensam ut etiam posteri ipsius
peccati sui maledictis obligarentur, beatis illis fra-
tribus multum longeque dissimilis, qui nuditatem
ipsam reverendi patris neque suis temerare ocu-
lis, neque alienis patere voluerunt, sed aversi, ut
scribitur, texerunt eum: quod est erratum sancti
viri nec approbasse nec prodidisse; atque idcirco
beata in posteros benedictione donati sunt. Sed
ad propositum redeamus.

Magno igitur metu nobis immutatae fidei ac
temeratae religionis piaculum pertimescendum
est; a quo nos solum constitutionis Ecclesiasticae disciplina, sed etiam censura Apostolicae
deterret auctoritatis. Scitum enim cunctis est
quam graviter, quam severe, quam vehementer invehatur in quosdam beatus Apostolus
Paulus, qui *mira levitate nimium cito translati
fuerant ab eo qui eos vocaverat in gratiam Christi,
in aliud Evangelium, quod non est aliud, qui coa-
cervarant sibi magistros ad sua desideria, a veritate
quidem auditum avertentes, conversi vero ad fabulas,
habentes damnationem quod primam fidem irri-
tam fecissent*; quos deceperant ii de quibus ad
Romanos fratres scribit idem Apostolus: *Rogo
autem vos, fratres, ut observetis eos qui dissentiones
et offendicula, praeter doctrinam quam ipsi didici-
stis, faciunt; et declinate ab illis. Hujusmodi enim
Christo Domino non serviunt, sed suo ventri, et
per dulces sermones et benedictiones seducunt corda*

their wrongdoing is doubly vicious: first, because they do not shrink from making others drink the poison of heresy; second, because, with a profane hand, they scatter like ashes already quenched the memory of some holy man and, by reviving his opinions, defame what ought to remain buried in silence. They thus follow the pattern of Ham, who not only failed to cover the nakedness of the venerable Noe, but even held it up to ridicule. Because of this violation of filial piety, therefore, he was considered so guilty that even his descendants inherited the malediction he incurred for his sin. Quite differently, his blessed brothers sought neither to profane with their own eyes nor to expose to others the nakedness of their venerable father. As it is written, they turned away and covered him, that is to say, they neither approved nor betrayed the fault of the saintly man, and for this they were rewarded with a happy benediction for their children. But let us return to our subject.

We should, therefore, dread with a great fear the sacrilege of changing faith and profaning religion. We should be deterred from such a sin not only by the discipline of ecclesiastical rule, but also by the censure of apostolic authority. For it is well known to all how heavily, how severely, how vehemently the blessed Apostle Paul attacks those who, with amazing levity, "are so quickly deserting him who called them to the grace of Christ, unto another gospel, which is not another" (Gal. 1:6–7); who, "according to their own desires had heaped to themselves teachers . . . and will turn away their hearing from the truth and will be turned unto fables" (2 Tim. 4:3–4), "having damnation because they have made void their first faith" (1 Tim. 5:12). They deceived those about whom the same Apostle writes to his Roman brothers: "Now I beseech you, brethren, to mark them who make dissentions and offenses contrary to the doctrine which you have learned, and avoid them. For they that are such do not serve Christ our Lord but their own belly; and by pleasing speeches

*innocentium. Qui intrant per domos, et captivas
ducunt mulierculas oneratas peccatis, quae ducuntur
variis desideriis; semper discentes, et ad scientiam
veritatis nunquam pervenientes. Vaniloqui et seduc-
tores, qui universas domos subvertunt, docentes quae
non oportet, turpis lucri gratia. Homines corrupti
mente, reprobi circa fidem, superbi, et nihil scientes,
sed languentes circa quaestiones et pugnas verborum;
qui veritate privati sunt, existimantes quaestum esse
pietatem: simul autem et otiosi discunt circumire
domos; non solum autem otiosi, sed et verbosi, et
curiosi loquentes quae non oportet: qui bonam con-
scientiam repellentes, circa fidem naufragaverunt:
quorum prophana vaniloquia multum proficiunt ad
impietatem, et sermo eorum ut cancer serpit.* Bene
autem quod de iis item scribitur: *Sed ultra non
proficient. Insipientia enim eorum manifesta erit
omnibus, sicut et illorum fuit.*

VIII

CUM ERGO TALES QUIDAM CIR-
cumeuntes provincias et civitates, atque
errores venalicios circumferendo, etiam ad
Galatas devenissent, cumque his auditis Gala-
tae nausea quadam veritatis affecti, Apostolicae
Catholicaeque doctrinae manna revomentes,
haereticae novitatis sordibus oblectarentur, ita
sese Apostolicae potestatis exeruit auctoritas,
ut summa cum severitate decerneret: *Sed licet
nos,* inquit, *aut angelus de caelo evangelizet vobis
praeterquam quod evangelizavimus vobis, anathema
sit* (Gal. 1). Quid est quod ait, Sed *licet nos?*
Cur non potius: *Sed licet ego?* Hoc est: *Etiamsi
Petrus, etiamsi Andreas, etiamsi Joannes, etiamsi
postremo omnis Apostolorum chorus evangelizet vobis*

and good words reduce the hearts of the innocent" (Rom. 16:17–18). "For of these sort are they who creep into houses and lead captive silly women laden with sins who are led away by diverse desires: ever learning and never attaining to the knowledge of the truth" (2 Tim. 3:6–7). "For there are also . . . vain talkers and seducers . . . who subvert whole houses, teaching things which they ought not, for filthy lucre's sake" (Titus 1:10–11), "proud, knowing nothing, but sick about questions and strifes of words, men corrupted in mind and who are destitute of the truth, supposing gain to be godliness" (1 Tim. 6:4–5). "And withal being idle, they learn to go about from house to house, and are not only idle but tattlers also and busybodies, speaking things which they ought not" (1 Tim. 5:13), "having . . . a good conscience, which some rejecting have made shipwreck concerning their faith" (1 Tim. 1:19); "profane and vain babblings, for they grow much towards ungodliness, and their speech spreadeth like a canker" (2 Tim. 2:16–17). What follows about them is equally well said: "But they shall proceed no farther, for their folly shall be manifest to all, as theirs also was" (2 Tim. 3:9).

8

SOME MEN OF THIS TYPE TRAVELING through provinces and cities, hawking their venal errors, came also to the Galatians. These, after having listened to the travelers, became lukewarm toward the truth, rejecting the manna of apostolic and Catholic doctrine and delighting in the dirt of heretical novelty. On this occasion, the authority of the apostolic power asserted itself and decreed with utmost severity: "But though we, or an angel from heaven, preach a gospel to you besides that which we have preached to you, let him be anathema" (Gal. 1:8). Why does he say: "But though we"? Why not rather: "But though I"? Because it is his understanding that even if Peter, or Andrew, or John, even, finally, if the whole community of Apostles "should preach a gospel to you

praeterquam quod evangelizavimus, anathema sit.
Tremenda districtio, propter adserendam pri-
mae fidei tenacitatem, nec sibi, nec ceteris coa-
postolis pepercisse! Parum est: *Etiamsi angelus,*
inquit, de caelo evangelizet vobis, praeterquam quod
evangelizavimus, anathema sit. Non suffecerat ad
custodiam traditae semel fidei, humanae conditionis commemorasse naturam, nisi angelicam
quoque excellentiam comprehendisset. Licet nos,
inquit, aut angelus de caelo. Non quia sancti
caelestesque angeli peccare jam possint; sed hoc
est quod dicit: Si etiam, inquit, fiat quod non
potest fieri, quisquis ille traditam semel fidem
mutare temptaverit, anathema sit.

Sed haec forsitan perfunctorie praelocutus est,
et humano potius effudit impetu, quam divina
ratione decrevit. Absit. Sequitur enim, et hoc
ipsum ingenti molimine iteratae insinuationis
inculcat: Sicut praediximus, et nunc iterum
dico: *Si quis vobis evangelizaverit, praeterquam quod*
accepistis, anathema sit. Non dixit: *Si quis vobis*
annuntiaverit praeterquam quod accepistis, benedictus
sit, laudetur, recipiatur; sed, anathema sit, inquit,
id est, separatus, segregatus, exclusus, ne unius ovis
dirum contagium innoxium gregem Christi venenata
permixtione contaminet.

IX

SED FORSITAN GALATIS ISTA TAN-
tum praecepta sunt. Ergo et illa solis Galatis
imperata sunt quae in ejusdem Epistolae sequenti-
bus commemorantur: qualia sunt haec: *Si vivimus*
spiritu, spiritu et ambulemus. Non efficiamur inanis
gloriae cupidi, invicem provocantes, invidentes, et
reliqua. Quod si absurdum est, et omnibus ex
aequo imperata sunt, restat ut sicut haec morum

other than that which we have preached to you, let them be anathema." What tremendous strictness! To assure firmness in the loyalty to the "first faith," he is ready to spare neither himself nor his fellow Apostles. But he is not satisfied with that, for his words are: Even if "an angel from heaven should preach a gospel to you besides that which we have preached to you, let him be anathema." For the preservation of the traditional faith, it was not sufficient for him to look only on the condition of human nature; he also included the eminent angelic nature. "Though we," he says, "or an angel from heaven." Not that he thinks the holy and celestial angels could sin. What he really means is: If that happened which cannot happen, let whosoever may attempt to change the traditional faith be anathema.

But, perhaps he pronounced these words incidentally, uttering them out of a quite human impulse rather than forming them under divine inspiration? This is far from the case. He continues, and emphasizes his point with the whole weight of reiterated assertion: "As we said before, so now I say again: If anyone preach to you a gospel besides that which you have received, let him be anathema" (Gal. 1:9). He did not say: "If anyone announced to you something besides that which you have received, let him be blessed, praised, welcomed," but: "let him be *anathema*." That is, let him be separated, segregated, excluded, so that the horrible contagion of a single sheep may not infect the innocent flock of Christ with its poisonous virus.

9

PERHAPS THOSE PRECEPTS ARE AIMED only at the Galatians? Then, other rules mentioned in later parts of the same Epistle would likewise be addressed only to the Galatians, as, for example: "If we live in the Spirit, let us also walk in the Spirit. Let us not be made desirous of vainglory, provoking one another, envying one another" (Gal. 5:25–26), and so on. But, if this is absurd, and if the rules are aimed equally at all, then it follows that,

mandata, ita etiam illa quae de fide cauta sunt
omnes pari modo comprehendant, et sicut nemini
licet invicem provocare aut invidere invicem, ita
nemini liceat, praeter id quod Ecclesia Catholica
usquequaque evangelizat accipere. Aut forsitan
tunc jubebatur, si quis annuntiasset praeterquam
quod annuntiatum fuerat, anathematizari; nunc
vero jam non jubetur. Ergo et illud quod item
ibi ait: *Dico autem, spiritu ambulate, et desiderium
carnis non perficietis*, tunc tantum jubebatur, modo
vero jam non jubetur. Quod si impium pariter et
perniciosum est ita credere, necessario sequitur
ut sicut haec cunctis aetatibus observanda sunt,
ita illa quoque quae de non mutanda fide sancita
sunt cunctis aetatibus imperata sint.

Annuntiare ergo aliquid Christianis catholicis, praeter id quod acceperunt nunquam licuit,
nusquam licet, nunquam licebit; et anathema-
tizare eos qui annuntiant aliquid praeterquam
quod semel acceptum est, nunquam non opor-
tuit, nusquam non oportet, nunquam non opor-
tebit. Quae cum ita sint, estne aliquis vel tantae
audaciae qui praeter id quod apud Ecclesiam
annuntiatum est annuntiet, vel tantae levitatis
qui praeter id quod ab Ecclesia accepit accipiat?
Clamat et repetendo clamat, et omnibus, et semper, et ubique per litteras suas clamat ille, ille
vas electionis, ille magister gentium, ille Apostolorum tuba, ille terrarum praeco, ille caelorum
conscius, ut si quis novum dogma annuntiaverit, anathematizetur. Et contra reclamant *ranae*
quaedam, et *cyniphes, et muscae moriturae*, quales
sunt Pelagiani, et hoc Catholicis: *Nobis*, inquiunt,
auctoribus, nobis principibus, nobis expositoribus,

equally with the moral commandments, those concerning faith apply to all in the same manner. Just as people are not permitted to provoke or envy one another, so no one is permitted to accept doctrines other than those the Catholic Church preaches everywhere. Or, perhaps it was an order only for that time that whosoever preached otherwise than had been taught [by the Apostles] be anathema, and that this order is now no longer valid? If this were true, then the exhortation, "But I say to them: Walk in the Spirit: and you shall not fulfill the lusts of the flesh" (Gal. 5:16), would likewise have been a command only for that time, and not for afterwards. But, if it is impious as well as perilous to think in this way, it follows logically that, so far as these rules are to be observed at any time, those concerning the immutability of holy faith also are orders which remain in force for all ages.

Consequently, to announce to Catholic Christians a doctrine other than that which they have received was never permitted, is nowhere permitted, and never will be permitted. It was ever necessary, is everywhere necessary, and ever will be necessary that those who announce a doctrine other than that which was received once and for all be anathema. If this be so, is there anyone alive so bold as to preach dogmas other than those taught by the Church, or so foolish as to accept doctrines besides those accepted by the Church? Crying aloud, crying aloud again and again and again, crying aloud to everyone, always and everywhere throughout his writings, is he, this "vessel of election" (Acts 9:15), this "doctor of the Gentiles" (1 Tim. 2:7), this trumpet among the Apostles, this herald of the earth, this heaven-conscious man; he is crying aloud that whoever announces a new doctrine is anathema. Against this voice there shout certain frogs and gnats and day flies,[29] such as the Pelagians, who have this to say to Catholics: We are the leaders, the chiefs, the interpreters. We tell

---

[29] By these names he compares the heretics to the plagues of Egypt narrated in Exod. 8. Eccles. 10:1 refers to "*muscae morientes*," dying flies.

damnate quae tenebatis, tenete quae damnabatis,
rejicite antiquam fidem, paterna instituta, majo-
rum deposita; et recipite: quaenam illa tandem?
horreo dicere: sunt enim tam superba, ut mihi
non modo afirmari, sed ne refelli quidem sine
aliquo piaculo posse videantur.

X

S ED DICET ALIQUIS: CUR ERGO
persaepe divinitus sinuntur excellentes quaedam personae in Ecclesia constitutae res novas
Catholicis annuntiare?

Recta interrogatio et digna quae diligentius atque uberius pertractetur: cui tamen non
ingenio proprio, sed divinae legis auctoritate,
Ecclesiastici magisterii documento satisfacien-
dum est. Audiamus ergo sanctum Moysen; et
ipse nos doceat cur docti viri, et qui propter
scientiae gratiam ab Apostolo etiam prophetae
nuncupantur, proferre interdum permittantur
nova dogmata, quae vetus Testamentum alle-
gorico sermone deos alienos appellare consue-
vit, eo quod scilicet ita ab haereticis ipsorum
opiniones sicut a gentibus dii sui observentur.
Scribit ergo in Deuteronomio beatus Moyses:
Si surrexerit, inquit, in medio tui propheta, aut qui
somnium vidisse se dicat (Deut. 13), id est, magister in Ecclesia constitutus, quem discipuli
vel auditores sui ex aliqua revelatione docere
arbitrentur. Quid deinde? *et praedixerit*, inquit,
signum atque portentum, et evenerit quod locutus est.
Magnus profecto nescio quis signatur magister
et tantae scientiae qui sectatoribus propriis non
solum quae humana sunt nosse, verum etiam
quae supra hominem sunt praenoscere posse
videatur; quales fere discipuli sui jactitant fuisse
Valentinum, Donatum, Photinum, Apollinarem,

you: Condemn what you adhered to; adhere to what you condemned; reject the ancient faith, the paternal institutions, the ancestral inheritance, and accept... After all, accept what? I shudder to say. It is so presumptuous that to refute it, let alone to utter it, is almost impossible without incurring some sort of sin.

10

THERE ARE SOME WHO WILL SAY: WHY, then, does Divine Providence often permit eminent persons, who are well established in the Church, to announce novel ideas to Catholics?

This is a good and earnest question, and should be thoroughly and extensively discussed. To do so satisfactorily, we have to refer not to our own ingenuity, but to the authority of divine Law and to the basic documents of ecclesiastical teaching. Let us listen, therefore, to blessed Moses. He himself may teach us why learned men and those who, because of their mysterious gifts, are called Prophets by the Apostles, sometimes are permitted to advance new dogmas. These are customarily called "strange gods" in the Old Testament, in accordance with its allegorical pattern of speech (and a very good term, incidentally, since the heretics have the same reverence for their own opinions as the Gentiles for their gods). Blessed Moses has this to say in Deuteronomy: "If there rise in the midst of thee a prophet or one that saith he hath dreamed a dream," that is, a doctor of the Church who, in the opinion of his disciples or listeners, is teaching by some revelation — well, what then? Moses continues: "and he foretell a sign and a wonder: and that come to pass which he spoke ... " Evidently, he has some outstanding master of great knowledge in mind, one who, in the eyes of his followers, is not only familiar with human affairs but also capable of a foreknowledge of transcendent matters — a master such as Valentine, Donatus, Photinus, Apollinaris, and the rest of them appeared to be in the opinion of their boasting

ceterosque ejusmodi. Quid postea? *Et dixerit,
inquit, tibi: Eamus, et sequamur deos alienos quos
ignoras, et serviamus eis.* Qui sunt *dii alieni*, nisi
errores extranei quos ignorabas, id est, novi et
inauditi? *Et serviamus eis*, id est, credamus eis,
sequamur eos. Quid ad extremum? *Non audies,*
inquit, *verba prophetae illius aut somniatoris.* Et
quare, oro te, a Deo non prohibetur doceri quod
a Deo prohibetur audiri? *Quia, inquit, temptat vos
Dominus Deus vester, ut palam fiat utrum diligatis
eum an non, in toto corde et in tota anima vestra.*

Luce clarius aperta causa est cur interdum
divina Providentia quosdam Ecclesiarum magistros nova quaedam dogmata praedicare patiatur. *Ut tentet vos*, inquit, *Dominus Deus vester.* Et
profecto magna temptatio est cum ille quem
tu prophetam, quem prophetarum discipulum,
quem doctorem et adsertorem veritatis putes,
quem summa veneratione et amore complexus
sis, is subito latenter noxios subinducat errores,
quos nec cito deprehendere valeas, dum antiqui
magisterii duceris praejudicio, nec facile dam-
nare fas ducas, dum magistri veteris praepediris
affectu.

XI

HIC FORSITAN EFFLAGITET ALI-
quis ut ea quae sancti Moysi verbis adserta
sunt, Ecclesiasticis aliquibus demonstrentur
exemplis. Aequa expostulatio, nec diu differenda.
Nam ut a proximis et manifestis incipiam, qualem fuisse nuper temptationem putamus, cum
infelix ille Nestorius, subito ex ove conversus in
lupum, gregem Christi lacerare coepisset, cum

disciples — well, and what then? "And he say to thee: Let us go and follow strange gods, which thou knowest not, and let us serve them . . . " (And who are the "strange gods," if not strange errors?) "Which thou knowest not," that is, novel and unheard-of ones. "And let us serve them," that is, let us have faith in them; let us follow them. And now, what is Moses' conclusion? "Thou shalt not hear the words of that prophet or dreamer," he says. And why, I ask you, does God not forbid to be taught what He forbids to be listened to? "For the Lord your God trieth you, that it may appear whether you love Him with all your heart, and with all your soul" (Deut. 13:1–3).

Clearer than daylight is the reason why Divine Providence sometimes suffers certain doctors of the Church to preach new dogmas: to the effect that "the Lord your God trieth you." And great is the temptation indeed when that man whom you look upon as a prophet, as a disciple of prophets, as a doctor and a defender of truth, whom you have embraced with highest veneration and love, suddenly and surreptitiously introduces noxious errors which you are unable to detect quickly so long as you still are under the spell of his former teaching, and which you do not dare to condemn easily so long as the affection for your old teacher hinders you from so doing.

11

HERE, SOMEONE PERHAPS MAY INSIST upon being given an illustration of the words of venerable Moses by a few examples from the history of the Church. We respond to this justifiable demand at once, and begin with recent and well-known events. How did the latest temptation come about, that this unfortunate man, Nestorius,[30] suddenly changed from a sheep into a wolf and began to harass the flock of Christ, while most

---

[30] Socrates (*Historia ecclesiastica* 7.29) deals more extensively with Nestorius. In 428, Nestorius, a priest of Antioch, was proclaimed, by Emperor Theodosius the Younger, Bishop of the See of Constantinople.

eum hi ipsi qui rodebantur ex magna adhuc
parte ovem crederent, ideoque morsibus ejus
magis paterent? Nam quis eum facile errare arbi-
traretur quem tanto Imperii judicio electum,
tanto sacerdotum studio prosecutum videret; qui
cum magno sanctorum amore, summo populi
favore celebraretur, quotidie palam divina tracta-
bat eloquia, et noxios quosque Judaeorum et
Gentilium confutabat errores? Quo tandem iste
modo non cuivis fidem faceret se recta docere,
recta praedicare, recta sentire, qui ut uni haeresi
suae auditum patefaceret, cunctarum haereseon
blasphemias insectabatur? Sed hoc erat illud
quod Moyses ait: *temptat vos Dominus Deus vester
si diligatis eum an non.*

Et ut Nestorium praetereamus, in quo plus
semper admirationis quam utilitatis, plus famae
quam experientiae fuit, quem opinione vulgi ali-
quamdiu magnum humana magis fecerat gratia
quam divina, eos potius commemoremus qui
multis profectibus multaque industria praediti
non parvae temptationi Catholicis hominibus exstiterunt. Velut apud Pannonias majorum memoria Photinus Ecclesiam Sirmitanam
temptasse memoratur: ubi cum magno omnium
favore in sacerdotium fuisset ascitus, et aliquandiu tamquam Catholicus administraret, subito,
sicut *malus ille propheta aut somniator* quem Moyses
significat, creditam sibi plebem Dei persuadere
coepit ut sequeretur deos alienos, id est, errores

of those who were bitten by him still believed in him as a sheep and were therefore the more exposed to the effects of his teeth? For who could readily consider entangled in error that man whom he saw elected after a judicious examination by the imperial court and honored by such deep affection on the part of the clergy, who was extolled by the holy men who loved him so much and by the people who gave him all their favor when in public he daily explained Holy Scripture and disclosed all the noxious errors of the Jews and Gentiles? How, then, could he fail to make everyone believe that he was teaching, preaching, and thinking orthodox truth—he who persecuted the blasphemies of all heresies in order to open the way for one heresy, his own?[31] This is precisely what Moses said: "The Lord your God trieth you that it may appear whether you love Him or not" (Deut. 13:3).

But, let us leave Nestorius, who excelled more by the admiration he created than by actual worth, more by reputation than by actual performance, and who for a time appeared great in public opinion less by divine grace than by natural cleverness. Let us rather remember those who, endowed with many outstanding qualities and great zeal, turned out to be serious temptations for Catholic people. Thus, for instance, Photinus[32] is still remembered by the older generation of Pannonia as the man who put the Church of Sirmium on trial. He had been admitted to the priesthood there with general approval, and then, having held his office for a while as a Catholic, suddenly, like that evil "prophet or dreamer" (as Moses called them), he began to persuade the people of God entrusted to him to follow "strange gods," that is, strange

---

[31] As Socrates (*Hist. eccles.* 1.1) bears witness, Bishop Nestorius, on the fifth day after his appointment, succeeded in his attempt to have the church of the Arians destroyed by fire. And, if we can trust Gothofredus, Nestorius was the author of that severe law enacted against the heretics by the emperor toward the end of May in that same year (*Cod. Theod.* 16.5,65).

[32] For Photinus, see above, ch. 2.

extraneos, quos antea nesciebat. Sed hoc usita-
tum. Illud vero perniciosum, quod ad tantum
nefas non mediocribus adminiculis utebatur.
Nam erat et ingenii viribus valens et doctrinae
opibus excellens et eloquio praepotens; quippe
qui utroque sermone copiose et graviter dispu-
taret et scriberet: quod monumentis librorum
suorum manifestatur, quos idem partim graeco,
partim latino sermone composuit. Sed bene quod
commissae ipsi oves Christi multum pro catholica fide vigilantes et cautae, cito ad praemo-
nentis Moysi eloquia respexerunt, et prophetae
atque pastoris sui licet admirarentur eloquentiam,
temptationem tamen non ignorarunt. Nam quem
antea quasi arietem gregis sequebantur, eumdem
deinceps veluti lupum fugere coeperunt. Neque
solum Photini sed etiam Apollinaris exemplo
istius Ecclesiasticae temptationis periculum
discimus, et simul ad observandae diligentius
fidei custodiam commonemur. Etenim ipse audi-
toribus suis magnos aestus et magnas generavit
angustias; quippe cum eos huc Ecclesiae traheret
auctoritas, huc magistri retraheret consuetudo;
cumque inter utraque nutabundi et fluctuantes,
quid potius sibi seligendum foret non expe-
dirent. Sed forsitan ejusmodi ille vir erat qui
dignus esset facile contemni. immo vero tantus
ac talis cui nimium cito in plurimis crederetur.
Nam quid illo praestantius, acumine, exercitatione, doctrina? Quam multas ille haereses
multis voluminibus oppresserit, quot inimicos
fidei confutaverit errores, indicio est opus illud
triginta non minus librorum, nobilissimum ac
maximum, quo insanas Porphyrii calumnias

errors formerly unknown to them. The case as such was
not unusual. What made it particularly pernicious was the
fact that he buttressed his nefarious undertaking with his
extraordinary qualities: his powerful genius, his excellent
education, and his outstanding eloquence. He used two
languages bluntly and forcibly for disputations and writings; proof of this is the number of his books, composed
partly in Greek, partly in Latin. Fortunately, the sheep of
Christ entrusted to him were watching and caring for the
Catholic faith and remembered in time the warnings of
Moses. Thus, they were not unaware of the temptation,
in spite of the admiration they had for the eloquence of
their prophet and pastor. As a matter of fact, by now they
began to shun as a wolf the very man they previously had
followed as the ram of the flock. Not only the example
of Photinus, but that of Apollinaris[33] as well, teaches us
the danger of temptation arising from churchmen; but
it likewise admonishes us to guard with great care the
observance of our faith. For he, too, caused his listeners
great trouble and deep anxiety. Drawn toward one side by
the authority of the Church and toward the other by the
influence of a master, wavering and fluctuating between
both, they did not know how to make up their minds.
Was this man, perhaps, the sort of person who could not
be but despised? Not at all. He was of such worth that, in
most respects, people trusted him only too readily. Who
was more outstanding than he in acuteness, versatility,
and erudition? How many heresies did he crush, in as
many volumes! How many errors dangerous to orthodoxy did he silence — as indicated by that work of no less
than thirty books, that eminent and outstanding work in
which he refuted with a mass of arguments the mad cal-
umnies of Porphyry![34] It would take too long to mention

---

[33] Accounts of Apollinaris may be found in Voisin, *L'Apollinarisme*
(Louvain, 1901) and Lietzmann, *Apollinaris von Laodicea und seine Schule*
(Tübingen, 1904).
[34] These books against Porphyry (d. 304) have been completely
destroyed.

magna probationum mole confudit. Longum
est universa ipsius opera commemorare; quibus
profecto summis aedificatoribus Ecclesiae par
esse potuisset, nisi prophana illa haereticae curiositatis libidine novum nescio quid adinvenisset
quo et cunctos labores suos velut cujusdam leprae
admixtione foedaret et committeret ut doctrina
ejus non tam aedificatio, quam temptatio potius
Ecclesiastica diceretur.

XII

HIC A ME FORSITAN DEPOSCA-
tur ut horum quos supra commemoravi
haereses exponam, Nestorii scilicet, Apollinaris,
et Photini. Hoc quidem ad rem de qua nunc agi-
mus non attinet. Propositum etenim nobis est,
non singulorum errores persequi, sed paucorum
exempla proferre, quibus evidenter ac perspicue
demonstretur illud quod Moyses ait, quia scilicet
si quando Ecclesiasticus aliquis magister, et ipse
interpretandis prophetarum mysteriis propheta,
novi quiddam in Ecclesiam Dei tentet inducere,
ad temptationem id nostram fieri Providentia
divina patiatur. Utile igitur fuerit, in excursu,
quid supra memorati haeretici sentiant breviter
exponere, id est, Photinus, Apollinaris, Nestorius.

Photini ergo secta haec est. Dicit Deum sin-
gulum esse et solitarium, et more Judaico con-
fitendum. Trinitatis plenitudinem negat, neque
ullam Dei Verbi aut ullam Spiritus sancti putat
esse personam. Christum vero hominem tantummodo solitarium adserit, cui principium adscribit
ex Maria: et hoc omnimodis dogmatizat, solam
nos personam Dei Patris et solum Christum
hominem colere debere. Haec ergo Photinus.

all his works, by which he could have been deemed an equal of the most constructive minds in the Church, if he had not, out of impious desire for heretical curiosity, invented some new doctrine or other which infected all his labors with a kind of leprosy and caused his teaching to become more a temptation than an edification in the Church.

12

A T THIS POINT, I MAY BE ASKED TO explain the heresies mentioned above, namely, those of Nestorius, Apollinaris, and Photinus. This matter, to be sure, is not directly related to the problem with which I am concerned. It is my purpose not to follow up the errors of individuals, but to bring out a few examples that give clear and convincing illustration of Moses's word that, if at any time a doctor of the Church—himself a prophet interpreting the mysteries of the Prophets—make the attempt to introduce some novelty into God's Church, Divine Providence admits this to test us. It will be useful, therefore, to develop the ideas of the aforementioned heretics only very briefly, in the form of a digression.

First, then, the doctrine of Photinus. According to him, God is singular and unique, and one has to conceive of Him in the manner of the Jews. He denies the plenitude of the Trinity and denies that there is either the Person of the Word or the Person of the Holy Spirit. As for Christ, he asserts that, though unique, He is merely a human being, and ascribes his origin to Mary. He states dogmatically that we must show reverence only to the Person of God the Father, but to Christ only as man. Thus Photinus.

Apollinaris vero in unitate quidem Trinitatis quasi consentire se jactitat, et hoc ipsum non plena fidei sanitate; sed in Domini incarnatione aperta professione blasphemat. Dicit enim in ipsa Salvatoris nostri carne aut animam humanam penitus non fuisse, aut certe talem fuisse cui mens et ratio non esset. Sed et ipsam Domini carnem non de sanctae Virginis Mariae carne susceptam, sed de caelo in Virginem descendisse dicebat; eamque nutabundus semper et dubius modo coaeternam Deo Verbo, modo de Verbi divinitate factam praedicabat. Nolebat enim in Christo esse duas substantias, unam divinam, alteram humanam, unam ex Patre, alteram ex matre; sed ipsam Verbi naturam putabat esse discissam, quasi aliud ejus permaneret in Deo, aliud vero versum fuisset in carnem; ut cum veritas dicat ex duabus substantiis unum esse Christum, ille contrarius veritati ex una Christi divinitate duas adserat factas esse substantias. Haec itaque Apollinaris.

Nestorius autem contrario Apollinari morbo, dum sese duas in Christo substantias distinguere simulat, duas introducit repente personas, et inaudito scelere duos esse vult filios Dei, duos Christos, unum Deum, alterum hominem, unum qui ex Patre, alterum qui sit generatus ex matre. Atque ideo asserit sanctam Mariam non Theotokon, sed Christotocon esse dicendam: quia scilicet ex ea non ille Christus qui Deus, sed ille qui erat homo, natus sit. Quod si quis eum putat in litteris suis unum Christum dicere et unam Christi praedicare personam, non temere credat. Aut enim istud fallendi arte machinatus est, ut per bona facilius suaderet et mala, sicut ait Apostolus: *Per bonum mihi operatus est mortem* (Rom. 7). Aut ergo, ut diximus, fraudulentiae causa quibusdam in locis

Apollinaris boasts of consenting to the doctrine of the Unity of the Trinity—though not in the full purity of the faith. But he blasphemes openly with regard to the Incarnation of our Lord. He says that there was no human soul in the body of our Saviour, or, if there were one, that it had neither mind nor reason. He asserts that the flesh of our Lord was not formed from the flesh of the Holy Virgin Mary, but descended from Heaven into the Virgin, and he taught, in constant wavering and doubt, sometimes that it was co-eternal with God the Word, sometimes that it was only created out of the divinity of the Word. He refused to admit two substances in Christ—one divine, the other human; one from the Father, the other from the mother. He believed that the Word's nature was itself divided, as though the one remained in God and the other had been converted into flesh. Whereas the Truth says that the one Christ consists of two substances, he—contrary to truth—asserts that from one Divinity of Christ two substances were made. This is the doctrine of Apollinaris.

Nestorius, who suffered from a disease quite contrary to that of Apollinaris, suddenly introduces two persons while pretending to distinguish two substances in Christ. In his unheard-of wickedness he assumes that there are two sons of God, two Christs—the one God, the other man; one, begotten of the Father, the other, of the mother. Thus he asserts that Holy Mary is not to be called *Theotokos* [Mother of God], but *Christotokos* [Mother of Christ], since she gave birth not to Christ-God, but to Christ-man. But, if one believes that he speaks in his writings of *one* Christ and that he teaches *one* Person of Christ, let him be careful not to give too easy credence to such an interpretation. Nestorius contrives this wording skillfully to deceive his readers—in order to recommend evil doctrines more easily through the intermediary of good ones, according to the words of the Apostle: "was that then which is good, made death unto me?" (Rom. 7:13). Well, either he deceitfully

scriptorum suorum unum Christum et unam
Christi personam credere se jactitat, aut certe
post partum jam Virginis ita in unum Christum
duas perhibet convenisse personas, ut tamen
conceptus seu partus Virginei tempore, et aliquanto postea duos Christos fuisse contendat;
ut cum scilicet Christus homo communis primum et solitarius natus sit, et necdum Dei
Verbo personae unitate sociatus, postea in eum
adsumentis Verbi persona descenderit; et licet
nunc in Dei gloria maneat adsumptus, aliquandiu tamen nihil inter illum et ceteros homines
interfuisse videatur.

XIII

HAEC ERGO NESTORIUS, APOL-
linaris, Photinus adversus Catholicam
fidem rabidi canes latrant: Photinus, Trinitatem
non confitendo; Apollinaris, convertibilem Verbi
dicendo naturam, et duas in Christo substantias
non confitendo, et aut totam Christi animam aut
certe mentem atque rationem in anima dene-
gando, et adserendo pro sensu mentis fuisse Dei
Verbum; Nestorius, duos Christos aut semper
esse, aut aliquandiu fuisse adseverando. Ecclesia
vero Catholica et de Deo et de Salvatore nostro
recta sentiens, nec in Trinitatis mysterio nec in
Christi incarnatione blasphemat. Nam et unam
divinitatem in Trinitatis plenitudine et Trinitatis aequalitatem in una atque eadem majestate
veneratur, et unum Christum Jesum, non duos,
eumdemque Deum pariter atque hominem confitetur. Unam quidem in eo personam, sed duas
substantias; duas substantias, sed unam credit

overemphasizes in certain passages of his writings that he believes in *one* Christ and *one* Person of Christ, or he pretends that, only after the birth from the Virgin, both Persons were united in *one* Christ; but this statement is made in such a way that it means that at the time of the Virgin's conception or bearing, and even for some time after, two Christs existed. Thus, though Christ, as merely man, was born the first, and unique, and not joined in unity of person to the Word of God, afterwards the Person of the Word descended into Him, assuming Him. Although now, having been assumed (by the Word), He abides in the glory of God, yet it would seem that for a time there was no difference between Him and other men.

13

THUS DO THESE MAD DOGS—NESTO-rius, Apollinaris, and Photinus—bark against the Catholic faith. Photinus denies the Trinity. Apollinaris declares that the nature of the Word is convertible; he does not recognize two substances in Christ; he says that Christ either has no soul at all or at least that there is no human mind and reason in His soul, and he asserts that the Word of God takes the place of that mind. Nestorius claims either that there are always two Christs or that for a time they were separated. But the Catholic Church, which has the true doctrine about God and our Saviour, does not blaspheme against either the mystery of the Trinity or the Incarnation of Christ. For it adores one Divinity in the plenitude of the Trinity and the equality of the Trinity in one and the same Majesty; and confesses one Jesus Christ, not two, the same Jesus Christ being at once God and man. The Church believes that there are in Him one Person, but two substances;[35] two substances, but

---

[35] That is, natures. Cf. Tertullian, *Adv. Prax.* 27: "Therefore is to be preserved the property of either substance, namely, that in Him the soul performed the acts proper to it, i.e., virtues, works, and signs, and the body functioned in its proper passions."

esse personam: duas substantias, quia mutabile
non est Verbum Dei, ut ipsum verteretur in carnem; unam personam, ne duos profitendo filios,
quaternitatem videatur colere, non Trinitatem.

Sed operae pretium est ut id ipsum etiam
atque etiam distinctius et expressius enucleemus.
In Deo una substantia, sed tres personae; in Christo duae substantiae, sed una persona. In Trinitate alius atque alius, non aliud atque aliud; in
Salvatore aliud atque aliud, non alius atque alius.
Quomodo in Trinitate alius atque alius, non aliud
atque aliud? Quia scilicet alia et persona Patris,
alia Filii, alia Spiritus sancti; sed tamen Patris
et Filii et Spiritus sancti non alia et alia, sed una
eademque natura. Quomodo in Salvatore aliud
atque aliud, non alius atque alius? Quia videlicet altera substantia divinitatis, altera humanitatis; sed tamen deitas et humanitas non alter et
alter, sed unus idemque Christus, unus idemque
filius Dei, et unius ejusdemque Christi et filii Dei
una eademque persona; sicut in homine aliud
caro, et aliud anima, sed unus idemque homo
anima et caro. In Petro et Paulo aliud anima,
aliud caro; nec tamen duo Petri, caro et anima;
aut alter Paulus anima, et alter caro; sed unus
idemque Petrus, unus idemque Paulus, ex duplici
diversaque subsistens animi corporisque natura.
Ita igitur in uno eodemque Christo duae substantiae sunt; sed una divina, altera humana;
una ex Patre Deo, altera ex matre Virgine; una
coaeterna et aequalis Patri, altera ex tempore et
minor Patre; una consubstantialis Patri, altera
consubstantialis matri; unus tamen idemque
Christus in utraque substantia. Non ergo alter
Christus Deus, alter homo; non alter increatus,
alter creatus; non alter impassibilis, alter passi-
bilis; non alter aequalis Patri, alter minor Patre;

one Person. Two substances because the Word of God is immutable so that it could not be converted into flesh; one Person, lest by acknowledging two Sons it seem to adore a quaternity instead of a trinity.

It is worthwhile to elaborate more distinctly and clearly on this point. In God there is one substance, but three Persons; in Christ, two substances, but one Person. In the Trinity there is distinction of Persons, but not of substance. In our Saviour there is distinction of substances, but not of Person. How is it that in the Trinity there is distinction of Persons, but not of substance? Because the Father is one Person, the Son, another, the Holy Spirit, a third. Yet, Father, Son, and Holy Spirit are not distinct in nature, but one and the same. Why in our Saviour is there a distinction of substances and not of Person? Because there is a divine substance and also a human substance. Yet, His Godhead and His humanity are not two persons, but one and the same Christ, one and the same Son of God, and one and the same Person of one and the same Christ and Son of God. So, in man, flesh and soul are differentiated, but soul and flesh are one and the same man. In Peter or Paul there is a distinction of soul and flesh, yet flesh and soul do not form two Peters, and there are not one Paul-soul and another Paul-flesh. But there are one and the same Peter and one and the same Paul, each of them consisting of a twofold and diverse nature of soul and body. Hence, there are also two substances in one and the same Christ, the one is divine; the other human; one is from God the Father, the other, from the Virgin Mother; one co-eternal and co-equal with the Father, the other temporal and less than the Father; one consubstantial with the Father, the other consubstantial with the Mother; yet one and the same Christ in either substance. Therefore, there is not one Christ-God and another Christ-man; not one uncreated and another created; not one impassible, the other passible; not one equal to the Father and the other less than the Father; not one from the Father and the

non alter ex Patre, alter ex matre; sed unus idemque Christus Deus et homo, idem non creatus
et creatus, idem incommutabilis et impassibilis,
idem commutatus et passus, idem Patri et aequalis et minor, idem ex Patre ante saecula genitus,
idem in saeculo ex matre generatus, perfectus
Deus, perfectus homo. In Deo summa divini-
tas, in homine plena humanitas. Plena, inquam,
humanitas: quippe quae animam simul habeat
et carnem, sed carnem veram, nostram, mater-
nam, animam vero intellectu praeditam, mente
ac ratione pollentem. Est ergo in Christo verbum,
anima, caro; sed hoc totum unus est Christus,
unus filius Dei, et unus Salvator ac Redemptor
noster. Unus autem, non corruptibili nescio qua
divinitatis et humanitatis confusione, sed integra et singulari quadam unitate personae. Neque
enim illa conjunctio alterum in alterum convertit
atque mutavit (qui est error proprius Arianorum),
sed ita in unum potius utrumque compegit, ut
manente semper in Christo singularitate unius
ejusdemque personae, in aeternum quoque
permaneat proprietas uniuscujusque naturae;
quo scilicet nec unquam Deus corpus esse inci-
piat, nec aliquando corpus, corpus esse desistat.
Quod etiam humanae conditionis demonstratur
exemplo. Neque enim in praesenti tantum, sed in
futuro quoque, unusquisque hominum ex anima
constabit et corpore, nec tamen unquam aut corpus in animam aut anima vertetur in corpus; sed
unoquoque hominum sine fine victuro, in unoquoque hominum sine fine necessario utriusque
substantiae differentia permanebit. Ita in Christo
quoque utriusque substantiae sua cuique in aeternum proprietas, salva tamen personae unitate,
retinenda est.

other from the Mother. But one and the same Christ is God and man; one and the same non-created and created; one and the same unchangeable and impassible *and* transformed and having suffered; one and the same co-equal with and less than the Father; one and the same begotten of the Father before time and born from a Mother in time — perfect God and perfect man; as God, highest divinity, as man, fullest humanity. I say fullest humanity, since He possesses both soul and flesh — true flesh, ours, from His mother, and a soul endowed with intelligence, possessing mind and reason. Hence, there is in Christ the Word, soul, flesh. But this whole is one Christ, one Son of God and for us one Saviour and Redeemer. He is One, not by some kind of corruptible mingling of divinity and humanity, but by an integral and unique unity of person. That conjunction neither converted nor changed one substance into the other — this is the characteristic error of the Arians.[36] Rather, both are united in such a way that, while singularity of one and the same Person always remains in Christ, the property of each Nature, on the other hand, endures for all eternity. Thus, God never begins to be a body, nor does the body ever cease to be body. The human condition offers a good illustration. For not only at present but also in the future, each individual does and will consist of body and soul. Never will either the body be converted into the soul or the soul into the body, but, in each individual destined to live without end, the differentiation of both substances will necessarily endure forever. So, also, in Christ the specific property that is characteristic for each of both substances will be retained forever, while the unity of person remains intact.

---

[36] Since the Arians denied that there was a human soul in Christ, they referred His Passion to His divinity. Since this took the place of the soul or substantive form in man, they said that in some manner it had been transformed into His humanity (see Hilary, *De Trinitate* 10.9 and 18: "But that the power and the nature of the Word might not be considered as lacking to Him in the flesh," etc.).

XIV

SED CUM PERSONAM SAEPIUS nominamus, et dicimus quod Deus per personam homo factus sit, vehementer verendum est ne hoc dicere videamur quod Deus verbum sola imitatione actionis quae sunt nostra susceperit, et quidquid illud est conversationis humanae, quasi adumbratus, non quasi verus homo fecerit; sicut in theatris fieri solet, ubi unus plures effingit repente personas, quarum ipse nulla est. Quotiescumque etenim aliqua suscipitur imitatio actionis alienae, ita aliorum officia aut opera patrantur, ut tamen hi qui agunt, non sint ipsi quos agunt. Neque enim (ut, verbi gratia, saecularium utamur exemplis), cum actor tragicus Sacerdotem effingit aut regem, sacerdos aut rex est. Nam desinente actu simul et ea quam susceperat persona desistit. Absit hoc a nobis nefarium scelestumque ludibrium. Manichaeorum sit ista dementia; qui phantasiae praedicatores, aiunt Filium Dei Deum, personam hominis non substantia extitisse, sed actu putativo quodam et conversatione simulasse.

Catholica vero fides ita Verbum Dei hominem factum esse dicit, ut quae nostra sunt, non fallaciter et adumbrate, sed vere expresseque susciperet, et quae erant humana, non quasi aliena imitaretur, sed potius ut sua gereret; et prorsus quod agebat, hoc etiam esset. Sicut ipsi nos quoque in eo quod loquimur, sapimus, vivimus, subsistimus, non imitamur homines, sed sumus. Neque enim Petrus et Joannes, ut eos potissimum nominem, imitando erant homines, sed subsistendo. Neque enim Paulus simulabat Apostolum, aut fingebat Paulum; sed erat Apostolus, et subsistebat Paulus. Ita etiam Deus Verbum adsumendo et habendo carnem, loquendo, faciendo, patiendo

14

A S WE RATHER FREQUENTLY USE THE term "Person" and declare that God became man "in person," we must take great care not to produce the impression that we mean that God the Word assumed our nature by mere imitation of our behavior and that He pursued His manner of life as an unreal and not as a true human being—as happens on the stage, where one individual in quick changes plays several parts without being identical with any of them. Each time that the behavior of other people is *imitated*, their reactions and actions are reproduced in such a way that those who are acting are not actually those whom they imitate. To use examples from secular plays, when an actor in a tragedy plays the part of a priest or king, he is not that priest or king; with the end of the play, the person he played ceases to exist. Far from me be such wicked and vicious mockery. We may leave madness like that to the Manichaeans, preachers of a phantasm, who declare that the Son of God, God Himself, did not exist in substance as a person, but that He simulated it by fictitious behavior and manner of life.

But the Catholic faith affirms that the Word of God was made man in such a way that He assumed our nature, not fallaciously and unreally, but in truth and reality; that He did not imitate human nature as being something different, but rather as His very own; furthermore, that He was that which He acted and whom He acted—precisely like ourselves, who, in so far as we speak, think, live, and exist, do not imitate, but actually are, human beings. Thus, Peter and John, to take such outstanding names, were men, not by imitation, but by subsistence. Similarly, Paul did not pretend to be an Apostle or feign to be Paul; he actually was the Apostle and subsisted as Paul. In the same way, also, God the Word deigned, by assuming and having a body, and by speaking, acting, and suffering through the

per carnem, sine ulla tamen suae corruptione
naturae, hoc omnino praestare dignatus est ut
hominem perfectum non imitaretur aut fingeret,
sed exhiberet, ut homo verus non videretur aut
putaretur, sed esset atque subsisteret. Igitur sicut
anima connexa carni, nec in carnem tamen versa,
non imitatur hominem, sed est homo, et homo
non per simulationem, sed per substantiam, ita
etiam Verbum Deus, absque ulla sui conversione,
uniendo se homini, non confundendo, non imitando factus est homo, sed subsistendo.

Abjiciatur ergo tota penitus personae illius
intelligentia quae fingendo imitatione suscipitur,
ubi semper alius est et aliud simulatur, ubi ille
qui agit, nunquam is est quem agit. Absit etenim
ut hoc fallaci modo Deus Verbum personam
hominis suscepisse credatur; sed ita potius ut
incommutabili sua manente substantia, et in se
perfecti hominis suscipiendo naturam, ipse caro,
ipse homo, ipse persona hominis existeret, non
simulatoria, sed vera, non imitativa, sed substan-
tiva, non denique quae cum actione desisteret,
sed quae prorsus in substantia permaneret.

XV

HAEC IGITUR IN CHRISTO PER-
sonae unitas nequaquam post Virginis
partum, sed in ipso Virginis utero compacta
atque perfecta est. Vehementer enim praecavere
debemus, ut Christum non modo unum, sed
etiam semper unum confiteamur: quia intole-
randa blasphemia est ut etiamsi nunc eum unum
esse concedas, aliquando tamen non unum, sed
duos fuisse contendas, unum scilicet post tem-
pus baptismatis, duos vero sub tempore nativi-
tatis. Quod immensum sacrilegium non aliter

flesh (without, however, any corruption of His own nature), to make it manifest that He did not imitate or feign but actually *presented* the perfect human being; so that He really was, and subsisted as, a true man, and did not merely seem nor was only believed to be such. Therefore, just as the soul united to the body (without, however, being converted into it) does not imitate man but *is* man — and this not by simulation but by substance — so was God the Word (without any conversion of Himself and not by confounding Himself with, but by uniting Himself to, man) made man, not by imitation, but substantially.

We must, therefore, completely reject any notion of "Person" that is built on fiction or imitation, on a permanent difference between being and pretending, and on the assumption that the acting individual never is the individual whom he represents. Let us get rid of the idea that God the Word assumed human personality in such a fallacious way. Let us rather realize that, His substance remaining immutable, He Himself existed as flesh, as man, as a person, when He assumed to Himself the nature of a perfect human being; that He existed so, not by simulation, but really, not by imitation, but substantially; and finally, that His existence did not cease with His acting, but remained permanently in its substance.

15

THUS, THIS UNITY OF THE PERSON IN Christ was formed and completed, not after the birth from the Virgin, but in the very womb of the Virgin. We must therefore take utmost care to be precise in our confession, so as to say that Christ is not merely *one*, but that He *always* has been *one*. Indeed, it would be an intolerable blasphemy to assert that, although you admit His now being one, you contend that He once was not one but two—one after His baptism, but two at the time of His birth. We cannot escape this enormous sacrilege unless we assert that humanity has been united to divinity through the unity

profecto vitare poterimus nisi unitum hominem
Deo, sed unitate personae, non ab ascensu, vel
resurrectione, vel baptismo, sed jam in matre,
jam in utero, jam denique in ipsa virginali con-
ceptione fateamur: propter quam personae unitatem indifferenter atque promiscue et quae Dei
sunt propria tribuuntur homini, et quae carnis
propria adscribuntur Deo. Inde est enim quod
divinitus scriptum est *et filium hominis descendisse de caelo, et Dominum majestatis crucifixum in
terra.* Inde etiam est ut carne Domini facta, carne
Domini creata, ipsum Verbum Dei factum, ipsa
sapientia Dei impleta, scientia creata dicatur;
sicut in praescientia manus ipsius et pedes ejus
fossi esse referuntur. Per hanc, inquam, personae
unitatem illud quoque similis mysterii ratione
perfectum est, ut carne Verbi ex integra matre
nascente, ipse Deus Verbum natus ex Virgine
catholicissime credatur, impiissime denegetur.

Quae cum ita sint, absit ut quisquam sanctam
Mariam divinae gratiae privilegiis et speciali gloria fraudare conetur. Est enim singulari quodam
Domini ac Dei nostri, Filii autem sui, munere
verissime ac beatissime Theotokos confitenda;
sed non eo modo Theotokos quo impia quaedam haeresis suspicatur, quae adserit eam Dei
matrem sola appellatione dicendam, quod eum
scilicet pepererit hominem qui postea factus est
Deus; sicut dicimus Presbyteri matrem, aut Episcopi matrem, non jam Presbyterum aut Episco-
pum pariendo, sed eum generando hominem qui
postea Presbyter vel Episcopus factus est. Non ita,
inquam, sancta Maria Theotokos, sed ideo potius
quoniam, ut supra dictum est, jam in ejus sacrato
utero sacrosanctum illud mysterium perpetra-
tum est, quod propter singularem quamdam
atque unicam personae unitatem, sicut Verbum
in carne caro, ita homo in Deo, Deus est.

of person, not through the ascension or resurrection or baptism, but within the Mother, in her womb, and—even more—in the virginal conception itself. Because of this unity of person, it happens that what is proper to God is ascribed to the man, and what is proper to the flesh is ascribed to God—indifferently and without distinction. Therefore, as it is written in Holy Scripture: "He that descended from heaven, the Son of man who is in heaven" (John 3:13) and "crucified the Lord of glory" (1 Cor. 2:8) on earth. Furthermore, since the body of the Lord was made and created, it is said that the "Word" of God Himself was "made" (John 1:14), His wisdom filled up (Eccl. 24:35), His knowledge created (Eccl. 1:4; 24:36); therefore do the prophetic writings refer to His hands and feet as "pierced" (Ps. 21:17). Through this unity of person it also becomes perfectly clear—by reason of a similar mystery—that it is most truly Catholic to believe (and most impious to deny) that the Word of God Himself was born from the Virgin even as the flesh of the Word was born from an Immaculate Mother.

Therefore, may God forbid that anyone should attempt to defraud holy Mary of her privileges of divine grace and of her special glory. For by a unique favor of our Lord and God she is to be confessed to be the most true and most blessed Mother of God (*Theotokos*). She is truly the Mother of God, not merely in name, as a certain impious heresy claims, because she gave girth to a man who later became God, as we call the mother of priests or bishops such, because she gave birth, not to a priest or a bishop, but to a child who later became one. Not thus, I say, is holy Mary the Mother of God, but rather because, as has already been said, in her sacred womb was accomplished the mystery that, by reason of a certain singular and unique unity of person, even as the Word is flesh in flesh, so the man is God in God.

XVI

S ED JAM EA QUAE SUPRA DE
memoratis haeresibus vel de catholica fide
breviter dicta sunt renovandae causa memoriae
brevius strictiusque repetamus; quo scilicet et
intelligantur iterata plenius, et firmius inculcata
teneantur.

Anathema igitur Photino non recipienti plenitudinem Trinitatis, et Christum hominem
tantummodo solitarium praedicanti. Anathema
Apollinari adserenti in Christo conversae divinitatis corruptionem, et auferenti perfectae
humanitatis proprietatem. Anathema Nestorio
neganti ex Virgine Deum natum, adserenti duos
Christos, et explosa Trinitatis fide, quaternitatem nobis introducenti.

Beata vero Catholica Ecclesia, quae unum
Deum in Trinitatis plenitudine et item Trinitatis aequalitatem in una Divinitate veneratur;
ut neque singularitas substantiae personarum
confundat proprietatem, neque item Trinitatis distinctio unitatem separet Deitatis. Beata,
inquam, Ecclesia, quae in Christo duas veras
perfectasque substantias, sed unam Christi
credit esse personam, ut neque naturarum
distinctio unitatem personae dividat, neque
item personae unitas differentiam confundat
substantiarum. Beata, inquam, Ecclesia, quae
ut unum semper Christum esse et fuisse fate-
atur, unitum hominem Deo, non post partum,
sed jam in ipso matris utero confitetur. Beata,
inquam, Ecclesia, quae Deum factum hominem
non conversione naturae, sed personae ratione
intelligit, personae autem non simulatoriae et
transeuntis, sed substantivae ac permanentis.
Beata, inquam, Ecclesia, quae hanc personae

16

IN ORDER TO REFRESH OUR MEMORY, let us more briefly and concisely repeat what we said about the above-mentioned heresies[37] and about the Catholic faith. By such a repetition, we may acquire a fuller understanding of and gain a firmer grasp on the matters already dealt with.

Anathema upon Photinus, who does not accept the plenitude of the Trinity and who teaches that Christ is merely man! Anathema upon Apollinaris, who asserts that the divinity had been transformed and corrupted in Christ and who takes away from Him the property of a perfect humanity! Anathema upon Nestorius, who denies that God was born from the Virgin, and who asserts that there are two Christs, thus introducing to us the quaternity after having destroyed the faith in the Trinity!

But blessed be the Catholic Church, which adores one God in the plenitude of the Trinity and the equality of the Trinity in one Divinity, so that neither the uniqueness of the substance confuses the individuality of the Persons, nor does the distinction of the Trinity differentiate the unity of the Divinity![38] Blessed, I say, be the Church, which believes that there are in Christ two real and perfect substances, but only one Person, so that neither the distinction of the natures divides the unity of the Person nor does the unity of the Person confuse the difference of the substances! Blessed, I say, be the Church, which confesses that Man was united to God, not after His birth, but even in the womb of His Mother, so that it thus makes clear that there always is, and always was, only Christ. Blessed, I say, be the Church, which recognizes that God was made man, not by a conversion of nature, but in virtue of the Person—not of a fictitious and transitory but of a substantial and permanent Person! Blessed, I say, be

---

[37] See chs. 12–14 above.
[38] Many things read either in this or in the preceding chapters may be found formulated most clearly in the Athanasian Creed.

unitatem tantam vim habere praedicat ut propter eam miro ineffabilique mysterio et divina
homini et Deo adscribat humana. Nam propter eam et hominem de caelo secundum Deum
descendisse non abnegat, et Deum secundum
hominem credit in terra factum, passum, et crucifixum. Propter ea denique et hominem Dei
filium et Deum filium Virginis confitetur. Beata
igitur ac veneranda, benedicta, et sacrosancta,
et omnino supernae illi angelorum laudationi
comparanda confessio, quae unum Dominum
Deum trina sanctificatione glorificat. Idcirco
etenim vel maxime unitatem Christi praedicat,
ne mysterium Trinitatis excedat.

Haec in excursu dicta sint, alias, si Deo pla-
cuerit, uberius tractanda et explicanda. Nunc
ad propositum redeamus.

XVII

DICEBAMUS ERGO IN SUPERIO-
ribus quod in Ecclesia Dei temptatio esset
populi, error magistri, et tanto major temptatio quanto ipse esset doctior qui erraret. Quod
primum Scripturae auctoritate, deinde ecclesiasticis docebamus exemplis, eorum scilicet
commemoratione qui cum aliquandiu sanae fidei
forent habiti, ad extremum tamen aut in alienam
decidissent sectam, aut ipsi suam haeresim con-
didissent. Magna profecto res, et ad discendum
utilis, et ad recolendum necessaria; quam etiam
atque etiam exemplorum molibus illustrare atque
inculcare debemus; ut omnes vere Catholici
noverint se cum Ecclesia doctores recipere, non
cum doctoribus Ecclesiae fidem deserere debere.

Sed ego ita arbitror, quod cum multos in
hoc temptandi genere proferre valeamus, nemo

the Church, which teaches that this unity of the Person
has such power that, because of it, by a wonderful and
ineffable mystery, divine action can be ascribed to man
and human action to God. For, because of that power, it
does not deny that man descended from heaven as God,
but also believes that on earth God was made, suffered,
and was crucified as man. Finally, because of that power,
she confesses the man as Son of God and God as the son
of the Virgin. Blessed, therefore, and revered, praised and
sacred and wholly worthy of that highest panegyric of the
angels, be the confession which glorifies one Lord God in
threefold sanctification! For that reason, this confession
proclaims the unity of Christ in such wise as not to deny
the mystery of the Trinity.

All these foregoing remarks were made in the form
of a digression. If it pleases God, these matters will be
treated and explained more fully at another time. Now
we return to our thesis.

17

WE SAID ABOVE[39] THAT IN THE CHURCH
of God the teacher's error was the people's temptation, and that the greater the erring teacher, the greater the
temptation. We made this clear, first, by the authority of
Holy Scripture, then, by examples taken from the history
of the Church that recalled to our mind the men who had
departed from their allegiance to sound faith and thus had
fallen into the doctrines of a strange sect or had founded
a heresy of their own. This is an important matter, indeed,
a useful experience, and to be remembered again and
again. We must insist on it and illustrate it by impressive
examples, so that all true Catholics may realize that they
should accept the teachers with the Church, and not desert
the faith of the Church with the teachers.

It is easy to produce innumerable instances of this kind
of temptation, but there is in my opinion scarcely a single

---

[39] Ch. 10.

paene sit qui Origenis temptationi valeat com-
parari; in quo plura adeo praeclara, adeo sin-
gularia, adeo mira exstiterunt, ut inter initia
habendam cunctis adsertionibus ejus fidem
quivis ille facile judicaret. Nam si vita facit auctoritatem, magna illi industria, magna pudici-
tia, patientia, tolerantia. Si genus vel eruditio,
quid eo nobilius saepius, ut ferunt, adfligeretur.
Neque vero haec in illo sola erant quae cuncta
postea temptationi forent, sed tanta etiam vis
ingemi, tam profundi, tam acris, tam elegantis
ut omnes paene multum longeque superaret;
tanta doctrinae ac totius eruditionis magnifi-
centia ut pauca forent divinae, paene fortasse
nulla humanae philosophiae quae non penitus
adsequeretur: cujus scientiae cum graeca con-
cederent, hebraea quoque elaborata sunt. Eloquentiam vero quid memorem, cujus fuit tam
amoena, tam lactea, tam dulcis oratio ut mihi
ex ore ipsius non tam verba quam mella quaedam fluxisse videantur? Quae non ille persuasu
difficilia disputandi viribus elimpidavit, quae
factu ardua non ut facillima viderentur effecit?
Sed forsitan argumentorum tantummodo nexi-
bus adsertiones suas texuit? Immo plane nemo
unquam magistrorum fuit qui pluribus divinae
legis uteretur exemplis. Sed, credo, pauca con-
scripsit? Nemo mortalium plura; ut mihi sua
omnia non solum non perlegi, sed ne inveniri
quidem posse videantur: cui ne quicquam ad
scientiae instrumenta deesset, etiam plenitudo
exabundavit aetatis. Sed forsitan discipulis

one comparable to that created by Origen. He had such
outstanding, such rare, such admirable qualities that, at
first sight, everyone was ready to accept all his statements
with a like trust. To judge from his way of life, great were
his zeal, his chastity, his patience, his endurance. With
regard to his family background and education, what can
be considered more noble than his birth into a family that
had become famous by martyrdom?[40] And, later on, after
he had lost for the cause of Christ not only his father but
also his whole fortune, [what was more admirable] than
his life in the bonds of holy poverty — a life in which he
so progressed as to suffer more than once (as we are told)
for having confessed the name of the Lord?[41] But these are
far from being all the traits that later would stimulate the
temptation. There still remain his powerful genius, so pro-
found, so acute, so subtle that he greatly surpassed almost
everyone, and his astounding knowledge and erudition, so
comprehensive that there were few matters in theology and
almost none in human philosophy that he did not master.
When he had gone through his studies in Greek, he took
up Hebrew.[42] And what shall I say of his eloquence? His
speech was so delightful, so fluid, so soft that it seems to
me it is honey rather than words that flows from his lips.
What difficult problems did he not clarify by the power
of his persuasive speech? What difficult facts did he not
present in a way easy to understand? Perhaps he built up
his statements by means of abstract reasoning? Not at all;
no other teacher made use of more examples taken from
divine Law. Or did he write only a few works? On the contrary; no mortal ever wrote more. It is quite impossible to
establish all his writings, not to speak of reading them all;
moreover, he became extremely old and thus could acquire

---

[40] Origen's father Leonidas suffered martyrdom in 202.

[41] Eusebius states that, in the persecution of Decius, Origen bore with
fortitude imprisonment, the rack, threats of torture by fire, and other
forms of suffering.

[42] For Origen's extraordinary skill in Greek and his knowledge of Hebrew,
see Jerome, *De viris illust.* 54, and Origen, *Hom. in Num.* 14.1.

parum felix? Quis unquam felicior? Nempe
innumeri ex sinu suo doctores, innumeri sacerdotes, confessores et martyres extiterunt. Jam
vero quanta apud omnes illius admiratio, quanta
gloria, quanta gratia fuerit, quis exsequi valeat?
Quis non ad eum paulo religiosor ex ultimis
mundi partibus advolavit? Quis Christianorum
non paene ut prophetam, quis philosophorum
non ut magistrum veneratus est? Quam autem
non solum privatae conditioni, sed ipsi quoque
fuerit reverendus imperio declarant historiae,
quae eum a matre eius, qui primus Romanorum
Principum Christianus fuit, Christiani magisterii auctoritate conscripsi. De cujus incredibili
quadam scientia si quis referentibus nobis Chri-
stianum non accepit testimonium, saltem testi-
ficantibus philosophis gentilem recipiat con-
fessionem. Ait namque impius ille Porphyrius
excitum se fama ipsius Alexandriam puerum
fere perrexisse, ibique eum vidisse jam senem,
sed plane talem tantumque qui arcem totius
scientiae condidisset.

Dies me citius defecerit quam ea quae in
illo viro praeclara exstiterunt vel ex minima
saltem parte perstringam: quae tamen omnia
non solum ad religionis gloriam, sed etiam ad
temptationis magnitudinem pertinebant. Quotus
enim quisque tanti ingenii, tantae doctrinae,
tantae gratiae virum aut facile deponeret, ac non
illa potius uteretur sententia, se cum Origene
errare malle, quam cum aliis vera sentire? et
quid plura? Eo res decidit ut tantae personae,

every scientific technique. Perhaps he had no influence over his disciples? Who ever had more? Innumerable were the doctors, priests, confessors, and martyrs who came from his school. Who can describe their admiration for him and the extent of his fame and influence? Who with any serious interest in religion did not rush to him from the most distant corners of the world? What Christian did not venerate him, almost as a prophet; what philosopher, as his master? History tells us how he was honored, not only by private persons but also by the court. The mother[43] of Emperor Alexander sent for him because of the divine wisdom with which he was endowed and with the love of which she also was burning. Another proof of his renown is the correspondence he addressed with the authority of a Christian teacher to Emperor Philip,[44] the first Christian among the Roman princes.[45] As for his almost incredible knowledge, if one does not accept our reference to Christian testimony, he may at least heed the statements made by pagan philosophers. The godless Porphyry says that, attracted by Origen's fame, he had gone as a young boy, to Alexandria, and that he saw him there—an old man of such extensive and deep wisdom that it seemed he had constructed a very fortress of universal knowledge.

It would take more than a whole day to describe, even briefly, all the outstanding qualities of the man. But the main point is that they not only tend to the glory of religion, but also indicate the magnitude of the temptation involved. For are there many who would pass by a man of such genius, such knowledge, such influence? Would they not rather make theirs the statement: "It is better to err with Origen than to be right with others?"[46] Why say more? The result was that not any ordinary human temptation but the exceedingly grave one of so great a personality,

---

[43] Julia Mamaea, who summoned him to Antioch.

[44] References to the letter from Origen to the Emperor Philip and to another written to his wife Severa are found in Eusebius, *Hist. eccl.* 6.36.3.

[45] Cf. Eusebius, *Chronicon ad annum* 247.

[46] Cf. Cicero, *Tusc. disp.* 1.17.39.

tanti doctoris, tanti prophetae, non humana aliqua, sed, ut exitus docuit, nimium periculosa temptatio plurimos a fidei integritate deduceret. Quamobrem hic Origenes tantus ac talis, dum gratia Dei insolentius abutitur, dum ingenio suo nimium indulget, sibique satis credit, cum parvi pendit antiquam Christianae Religionis simplicitatem, dum se plus cunctis sapere prae-sumit, dum ecclesiasticas traditiones et veterum magisteria contemnens, quaedam Scripturarum capitula novo more interpretatur, meruit ut de se quoque Ecclesiae Dei diceretur: *Si surrexerit in medio tui propheta.* Et paulo post: *Non audies,* inquit, *verba prophetae illius.* Et item: *Quia temptat vos,* inquit, *Dominus Deus vester utrum diligatis eum an non.* Vere non solum temptatio, sed etiam magna temptatio deditam sibi atque in se pen-dentem Ecclesiam admiratione ingenii, scientiae, eloquentiae, conversationis, et gratiae, nihil de se suspicantem, nihil verentem, subito a veteri Religione in novam prophanitatem sensim pau-latimque traducere.

Sed dicet aliquis corruptos esse Origenis libros. Non resisto; quin potius et malo. Nam id a quibusdam et traditum et scriptum est, non Catholicis tantum, verum etiam Haereticis. Sed illud est quod nunc debemus advertere etsi non ipsum, libros tamen sub nomine suo editos, magnae esse temptationi: qui multis blasphe-miarum vulneribus scatentes, non ut alieni, sed quasi sui et leguntur et amantur; ut etsi in errore concipiendo Origenis non fuit sensus, ad erro-rem tamen persuadendum Origenis auctoritas valere videatur.

so prominent a doctor, so influential a prophet, turned masses of people away from the integrity of the faith, as later events made clear.[47] Hence, to the same Origen, great and outstanding as he was, should be applied the words addressed to the Church of God: "If there rise in the midst of thee a prophet," and a little later on, "thou shalt not hear the words of that prophet," and again, "for the Lord your God trieth you, whether you love Him or not" (Deut. 13:1–3). And this, because he arrogantly abused the grace of God; because he set too much store on his own ability and relied too much on himself, neglecting the old simplicity of the Christian religion; because he presumed to know more than all the others; because he despised ecclesiastical traditions and the teachings of the fathers and interpreted some passages of Holy Scripture in a novel manner.[48] Indeed, it is not an ordinary, it is a very great trial that the Church which was devoted to and depended upon him out of admiration for his genius, his knowledge, his eloquence, his manner of life and his influence — that the Church which had no suspicion and feared nothing for itself — was suddenly endangered by being gradually turned away from the old religion to a modern heresy.

Someone may object and say that Origen's writings were falsified.[49] I do not oppose this idea; I would prefer that it were so. Indeed, several people, Catholics as well as heretics, have orally and in writing asserted the truth of this conjecture. But the point we must emphasize is that the books published under his name, even if he were not their author, are the cause of serious temptation. Abounding in deadly blasphemies, they are read and loved, not as books by someone else, but as *his* writings, so that on Origen's authority they have the power to persuade their readers to error, even if this were not his intention.

---

[47] As to the disputes about Origen that arose at the end of the fourth century between the bishops and the monks of Egypt, we have, as it were, an eyewitness in Sulpicius Severus, *Dial.* 1.6.

[48] Origen emphasized unduly the allegorical interpretation.

[49] Origen complained that his writings had been falsified by the heretics, and many later on made a similar charge, e.g., Sulpicius Severus, *Dial.* 1.6.

XVIII

SED ET TERTULLIANI QUOQUE
eadem ratio est. Nam sicut ille apud Graecos,
ita hic apud Latinos nostrorum omnium facile
princeps judicandus est. Quid enim hoc viro
doctius, quid in divinis atque humanis rebus
exercitatius? Nempe omnem philosophiam et
cunctas philosophorum sectas, auctores, adser-
toresque sectarum, omnesque eorum disciplinas,
omnem historiarum ac studiorum varietatem
mira quadam mentis capacitate complexus est.
Ingenio vero nonne tam gravi ac vehementi
excelluit ut sibi nihil paene ad expugnandum
proposuerit quod non aut acumine inruperit,
aut pondere eliserit? Jam porro orationis suae
laudes quis exsequi valeat, quae, tanta nescio
qua rationum necessitate concerta est ut ad consensum sui quos suadere non potuerit impel-
lat; cujus quot paene verba, tot sententiae sunt;
quot sensus, tot victoriae. Sciunt hoc Marciones,
Apelles, Praxeae, Hermogenes, Judaei, Gentiles,
Gnostici, ceterique; quorum ille blasphemias
multis ac magnis voluminum suorum molibus,
velut quibusdam fulminibus, evertit.

Et tamen hic quoque post haec omnia, hic,
inquam, Tertullianus, catholici dogmatis, id
est, universalis ac vetustae fidei parum tenax,
ac disertior multo quam felicior, mutata deinceps sententia, fecit ad extremum quod de eo
beatus confessor Hilarius quodam loco scribit:
Sequenti, inquit, errore detraxit scriptis probabili-
bus auctoritatem. Et fuit ipse quoque in Ecclesia
magna temptatio. Sed de hoc nolo plura dicere.

18

QUITE SIMILAR, ALSO, IS THE CASE OF Tertullian. For, as Origen among the Greeks, so must Tertullian among the Latins clearly be considered as supreme. Who was more scholarly than this man, and who better trained in divine and human matters? With his amazing mental capacity he actually embraced the entire range of philosophy, including all particular schools, their heads, disciples, and systems, as well as the manifold forms of historical and natural sciences. Did his outstanding genius not possess such vigor and impetus that whatever he was attacking was either caught by the keenness or crushed by the weight of his mind? No one is able adequately to evaluate and to praise his eloquence. The logical nexus of his argumentation was so closely knit that he forced those whom he could not persuade to adhere to his point of view.[50] Almost each word of his is a thought, and each sentence a victory. They all experienced it—the followers of Marcion, Apelles, Praxias, Hermogenes, the Jews, the Gentiles, the Gnostics, and so many others whose blasphemies he demolished with many and weighty books, as though by lightning.

Yet this same Tertullian was, after all, not steadfast enough in Catholic dogma, the universal and traditional faith. He was more eloquent than faithful,[51] and thus ended in changing his position, precisely as the blessed confessor Hilary said of him: "By his subsequent error he deprived his commendable writings of their authority."[52] So, too, he turned out to be a great temptation to the Church. But I do not wish to say more about this case. Only one point

---

[50] Cf. Augustine, *De haer.* 86, Lactantius, *Inst. div.* 5.1.23, and Jerome, *Epist.* 58.10; 48.13.
[51] The text in the four codices reads *fidelior*; but all later editors, with Sichardus and Costerius, have *felicior*.
[52] *Commentary on St. Matthew* 5.1.

Hoc tantum commemorabo, quod contra Moysi praeceptum exsurgentes in Ecclesia novellas Montani furias et insana illa insanarum mulierum novitii dogmatis somnia veras prophetias adseverando, meruit ut de se quoque et scripturis suis diceretur: *Si surrexerit in medio tui propheta.* Et mox: *Non audies verba prophetae illius.* Quare? *Quia*, inquit, *temptat vos Dominus vester utrum diligatis eum an non.*

XIX

HIS IGITUR TOT AC TANTIS ceterisque ejusmodi Ecclesiasticorum exemplorum molibus evidenter advertere, et secundum Deuteronomii leges luce clarius intelligere debemus, quod si quando aliquis Ecclesiasticus magister a fide aberraverit, ad temptationem id nostram fieri Providentia divina patiatur, utrum diligamus Deum an non in toto corde et in tota anima nostra.

XX

QUAE CUM ITA SINT, ILLE EST verus et germanus Catholicus qui veritatem Dei, qui Ecclesiam, qui Christi corpus diligit, qui divinae Religioni, qui catholicae fidei nihil praeponit, non hominis cujuspiam auctoritatem, non amorem, non ingenium, non eloquentiam, non philosophiam; sed haec cuncta despiciens, et in fide fixus, stabilis, permanens, quicquid universaliter antiquitus Ecclesiam Catholicam tenuisse cognoverit, id solum sibi tenendum credendumque decernit; quicquid vero ab aliquo deinceps uno praeter omnes vel contra omnes sanctos novum et inauditum subindici senserit, id non ad

may be added. When the modern madness of Montanus and the foolish imaginings of ridiculous women[53] about a new dogma arose in the Church, he declared them to be true prophecies — contrary to Moses's advice. Hence, he richly deserved that it also ought to be said of him and his writings: "If there rise in the midst of thee a prophet thou shalt not hear the words of that prophet." And why not? "For," it is said, "the Lord your God trieth you whether you love Him or not" (Deut. 13:1–3).

19

BY VIRTUE OF THESE MANY CONVINC-ing examples from Church history, and others of the same kind, we must clearly perceive and, according to the rules of Deuteronomy, fully understand that, if at any time a teacher of the Church deviates from the faith, Divine Providence permits this to happen in order to test and to try us, "whether we love God, or not, with all our heart and all our soul" (Deut. 13:3).

20

SINCE THIS IS SO, WE MAY SAY THAT A true and genuine Catholic is the man who loves the Truth of God, the Church, and the Body of Christ (Eph. 1:23); who does not put anything above divine religion and the Catholic faith—neither the authority, nor the affection, nor the genius, nor the eloquence, nor the philosophy of any other human being. He despises all that and, being firmly founded in the faith, is determined to hold and believe nothing but what the Catholic Church, as he has perceived, has held universally and from ancient times. He is one who comprehends that any kind of modern and sensational doctrine, introduced by someone outside of and contrary to the position taken by the saints, does not

---

[53] Priscilla and Maximilla.

Religionem sed ad temptationem potius intelligit pertinere, tum praecipue beati Apostoli Pauli eruditus eloquiis: hoc est enim quod in prima ad Corinthios Epistola scribit: *Oportet,* inquit, *et haereses esse, ut probati manifesti fiant in vobis;* ac si diceret: Ob hoc haereseon non statim divinitus eradicantur auctores, ut probati manifesti fiant, id est, ut unusquisque quam tenax et fidelis et fixus catholicae fidei sit amator appareat.

Et revera, cum quaeque novitas ebullit, statim cernitur frumentorum gravitas et levitas palearum; tunc sine magno molimine excutitur ab area quod nullo pondere intra aream tenebatur. Namque alii illico prorsus avolant; alii vero tantummodo excussi, et perire metuunt, et redire erubescunt saucii, semineces ac semivivi; quippe qui tantam veneni hauserint quantitatem quae nec occidat nec digeratur, nec mori cogat nec vivere sinat, heu miseranda conditio! quantis illi curarum aestibus, quantis turbinibus exagitantur? Nunc etenim, qua ventus impulerit, incitato errore rapiuntur; nunc in semetipsos reversi, tamquam contrarii fluctus, reliduntur, nunc temeraria praesumptione et ea quae incerta videntur adprobant; nunc irrationali metu, etiam quae certa sunt expavescunt; incerti qua eant, qua redeant, quid adpetant, quid fugiant, quid teneant, quid dimittant. Quae quidem dubii et male penduli cordis afflictio divinae erga se miserationis est medicina, si sapiant.

Idcirco etenim extra tutissimum catholicae fidei portum diversis cogitationum quatiuntur, verberantur, ac paene enecantur procellis, ut excussa in altum elatae mentis vela deponant, quae male novitatum ventis expanderant,

pertain to religion, but rather constitutes a temptation, according to the words he has learned from the blessed Apostle Paul, who has this to say: "For there must also be heresies, that they who are approved may be made manifest among you" (1 Cor. 11:19). It is as if the Apostle meant: The authors of heresies are not instantly rooted out by God, in order to make manifest those who are approved, that is, in order to make evident to what degree each one is a steadfast, faithful, and firm lover of the Catholic faith.

Indeed, as soon as some novelty is stirred up, the wheat and the chaff are immediately separated from each other by their respective heaviness and lightness (Matt. 3:12); what for lack of weight cannot be held within the threshing floor is then easily fanned away. Some fly off instantly; others, only shaken up, fear to perish and are ashamed to return—hurt, half-dead and half-alive, since they have devoured a quantity of poison (not enough to kill, but too much to be digested), a quantity that does not necessarily bring with it death, yet does not permit them really to live. What a miserable situation! In what anxieties do they linger! By what whirlwinds are they harassed! Sometimes, stirred up by an error, they are tossed wherever the wind drives them; sometimes they turn back on themselves as though driven by countercurrents. Now they approve with arbitrary presumption what seems to be uncertain; now, under the pressure of an irrational fear, they are in dread of even the most certain truths—never being sure where to go, where to return, what to desire, what to avoid, what to hold, what to give up. If only they would understand that what they are suffering in their wavering and unbalanced hearts is the medicine which the divine compassion has prepared for them!

As a matter of fact, being outside the completely secure harbor of the Catholic faith, they are harassed, beaten, and, as it were, slain, by the onslaughts of opposing ideas. Under their impact, they may furl the sails of their puffed-up minds which they had guiltily spread in the wind of novelty; they

seseque intra fidissimam stationem placidae ac
bonae matris reducant et teneant, atque amaros
illos turbulentosque errorum fluctus primitus
revomant, ut possint deinceps vivae et salientis
aquae fluenta potare. Dediscant bene quod didi-
cerant non bene; et ex toto Ecclesiae dogmate
quod intellectu capi potest capiant, quod non
potest credant.

XXI

QUAE CUM ITA SINT, ITERUM
atque iterum eadem mecum revolvens et
reputans, mirari satis nequeo tantam quorum-
dam hominum vesaniam, tantam excaecatae
mentis impietatem, tantam postremo errandi
libidinem ut contenti non sint tradita semel et
accepta antiquitus credendi regula, sed nova
ac nova in diem quaerant, semperque aliquid
gestiant Religioni addere, mutare, detrahere;
quasi non caeleste dogma sit quod semel
revelatum esse sufficiat, sed terrena institutio,
quae aliter perfici nisi assidua emendatione,
immo potius reprehensione non possit, cum
divina clament oracula: *Ne transferas terminos
quos posuerunt patres tui*; et: *Super judicantem ne
judices*; et*: Scindentem sepem mordebit eum ser-
pens*, et illud apostolicum, quo omnes omnium
haereseon sceleratae novitates velut quodam
spiritali gladio saepe truncatae semperque
truncandae sunt: *O Timothee, depositum custodi,
devitans prophanas vocum novitates et oppositiones
falsi nominis scientiae, quam quidam promittentes,
circa fidem exciderunt.*

Et post haec inveniuntur aliqui tanta invete-
ratae frontis duritia, tanta impudentiae incude,

may return to and stay within that most trustworthy resting place of their gentle and kind mother; they may disgorge those bitter and stormy floods of error, and, finally, be able to drink of the streams of "living water springing up (into life everlasting)" (John 4:10,14). They may well unlearn what they had badly learned; they may grasp as much of the whole dogma of the Church as can be intellectually understood, and accept in faith[54] what cannot be understood.

21

SINCE THIS IS SO, I AM MOVED TO reflect and ponder again and again. I cannot help wondering about such madness in certain people, the dreadful impiety of their blinded minds, their insatiable lust for error that they are not content with the traditional rule of faith as once and for all received from antiquity, but are driven to seek another novelty daily. They are possessed by a permanent desire to change religion, to add something and to take something away—as though the dogma were not divine, so that it has to be revealed only once. But they take it for a merely human institution, which cannot be perfected except by constant emendations, nay rather, by constant corrections. Yet the divine prophecies say: "Pass not beyond the ancient bounds which thy fathers have set" (Prov. 22:28) and "Judge not against a judge" (Eccl. 8:17) and "he that breaketh a hedge, a serpent shall bite him" (Eccl. 10:8). And we have this word of the Apostle that like a spiritual sword has often slaughtered and will forever slaughter all the vicious novelties of all the heretics: "O Timothy, keep that which is committed to thy trust, avoiding the profane novelties[55] of words and oppositions of knowledge falsely so called, which some promising have erred concerning the faith" (1 Tim. 6:20–21).

Are there really people who can listen to such adjurations and then remain in such hardened and shameless

---

[54] Cf. Augustine, *De Trinitate* 7, end.
[55] In Greek, *kenophonías*.

tanto adamante pertinaciae, qui tantis elo-
quiorum caelestium molibus non succumbant,
tantis ponderibus non fatiscant, tantis malleis
non conquassentur, tantis postremo fulminibus non conterantur? *Devita*, inquit, *prophanas
vocum novitates*: Non dixit antiquitates, non
dixit vetustates; immo plane quid e contrario
sequeretur ostendit. Nam si vitanda est novitas,
tenenda est antiquitas; et si prophana est novitas, sacrata est vetustas. *Et oppositiones*, inquit,
falsi nominis scientiae. Vere falsum nomen apud
doctrinas Haereticorum; ut ignorantia scientiae, et caligo serenitatis, et tenebrae luminis
appellatione fucentur. *Quam quidam*, inquit,
promittentes, *circa fidem exciderunt*. Quid promittentes exciderunt, nisi novam nescio quam
ignoratamque doctrinam?

Audias etenim quosdam ipsorum dicere:
*Venite, o insipientes et miseri, qui vulgo Catholici
vocitamini, et discite fidem veram, quam praeter
nos nullus intelligit, quae multis ante saeculis latuit,
nuper vero revelata et ostensa est; sed discite furtim
atque secretim: delectabit enim vos.* Et item*: Cum
didiceritis, latenter docete; ne mundus audiat, nec
Ecclesia sciat: paucis namque concessum est tanti
mysterii capere secretum.* Nonne haec verba sunt
illius *meretricis* quae apud Salomonis Prover-
bia *vocat ad se praetereuntes viam qui dirigunt iter
suum*? *Qui est*, inquit, *vestrum insipientissimus,
divertat ad me.* Inopes autem sensu exhortatur
dicens: *Panes occultos libenter attingite, et aquam
dulcem furtim bibite.* Quid deinde? *At ille*, inquit,
nescit quoniam terrigenae apud eam pereunt. Qui
sunt isti *terrigenae*? Exponat Apostolus: *Qui
circa fidem*, inquit, *exciderunt.*

stubbornness, such stony impudence, such adamant obstinacy, as not to yield to the mighty weight of these divine words and to weaken under such a load, as not to be shattered by these hammer strokes, as not to be crushed by such powerful thunderbolts? "Avoiding," he says, "profane novelties of words." He did not say "antiquities" or "the old traditions." No, he clearly shows the positive implications of this negative statement: Novelty is to be avoided, hence, antiquity has to be respected; novelty is profane, hence, the old tradition is sacred. "And," he continues, "the oppositions of knowledge falsely so called." A misnomer indeed for the doctrines of the heretics — ignorance beautified by the name of knowledge, darkness by that of clarity, night by that of light! "Which some promising have erred concerning the faith." What did they promise, and in what did they err, if not in regard to a hitherto unknown doctrine?

You may hear it said by some of these [heretics]: "Come, you poor ignorant people, commonly called Catholics, and learn the true faith which no one knows except ourselves, which was concealed for many centuries, but which lately has been revealed and made manifest. But learn it furtively and secretly; it will delight you. And when you have learned it, teach it covertly, lest the world hear it or the Church find out about it. For it is given only to a few to receive the secret of so great a mystery." Are not these the words of that harlot, who, in the Proverbs of Solomon, "calls them that pass by the way and go on their journey"? "He," she says, "that is a little one, let him turn to me." And she invites fools, in the words: "Stolen waters are sweeter, and hidden bread is more pleasant." And how does the author continue? He says: "But he did not know that her guests are in the depths of hell" (Prov. 9:15–18). Who are these guests? Let the Apostle explain it to us: they are those "who have erred concerning the faith" (1 Tim. 6:21).

XXII

S ED OPERAE PRETIUM EST
totum ipsum Apostoli capitulum diligentius
pertractare. *O Timothee*, inquit, *depositum custodi,
devitans profanas vocum novitates.*

O! Exclamatio ista et praescientiae est pariter
et charitatis. Praevidebat enim futuros, quos
etiam praedolebat, errores. Quis est hodie
Timotheus nisi vel generaliter universa Ecclesia, vel specialiter totum corpus Praeposito-
rum, qui integram divini cultus scientiam vel
habere ipsi debent vel aliis infundere? Quid
est, *depositum custodi*? *Custodi*, inquit, *propter
fures, propter inimicos, ne dormientibus hominibus,
superseminent zizania super illud tritici bonum
semen quod seminaverat filius hominis in agro suo.
Depositum*, inquit, *custodi.* Quid est *depositum*?
id est, quod *tibi creditum est, non quod a te inven-
tum; quod accepisti, non quod excogitasti; rem non
ingenii, sed doctrinae, non usurpationis privatae, sed
publicae traditionis; rem ad te perductam, non a te
prolatam: in qua non auctor debes esse, sed custos;
non institutor, sed sectator; non ducens, sed sequens.
Depositum*, inquit, *custodi*; *catholicae fidei talen-
tum inviolatum illibatumque conserva. Quod tibi
creditum, hoc penes te maneat, hoc a te tradatur.
Aurum accepisti, aurum redde: nolo mihi pro aliis
alia subjicias: nolo pro auro aut impudenter plum-
bum aut fraudulenter aeramenta supponas: nolo auri
speciem, sed naturam plane.*

*O Timothee, O Sacerdos, O Tractator, O Doc-
tor, si te divinum munus idoneum fecerit, ingenio,*

22

IT IS WORTHWHILE TO STUDY THE whole text of the Apostle more thoroughly. "O Timothy," he says, "keep that which is committed to thy trust, avoiding the profane novelties of words" (1 Tim. 6:20).

The exclamation "O" is at one and the same time an expression of foreknowledge and of love. He foresaw future errors and suffered pain in advance over their coming. The Timothy of today is either, speaking generally, the Universal Church, or, in particular, the whole body of ecclesiastical superiors who ought to have for themselves and to administer to the people an integral knowledge of divine worship. What, then, does "keep that which is committed to thee" mean? "Keep it," he says, in the face of thieves and enemies, lest while men are asleep, they oversow cockle among the good wheat which the Son of man had sown in His field (Matt. 13:24ff.). "Keep that which is committed." What is "committed"? It is that which has been entrusted to you, not that which you have invented; what you have received, not what you have devised; not a matter of ingenuity, but of doctrine; not of private acquisition, but of public tradition; a matter brought to you, not created by you; a matter you are not the author of, but the keeper of; not the teacher, but the learner; not the leader, but the follower. This deposit, he says, guard. Preserve the "talent" (Matt. 25:15) of the Catholic faith unviolated and unimpaired. Let what has been entrusted to you remain with you, let it be handed down by you. You received gold; hand it down as gold. I do not want you to substitute one thing for another; I do not want you shamelessly to put lead, or, deceitfully, copper, in the place of gold. I do not want something that resembles gold, but real gold.

O Timothy, O priest, O interpreter,[56] O doctor, if a gift of heaven has prepared you by mental power, experience,

---

[56] This term, introduced by the writers of that time, means one who explains, or a teacher (see ch. 28).

exercitatione, doctrina, esto spiritalis tabernaculi Beseleel, pretiosas divi dogmatis gemmas exsculpe, fideliter coapta, adorna sapienter, adjice splendorem, gratiam, venustatem. Intelligatur, te exponente illustrius, quod ante obscurius credebatur. Per te posteritas intellectum gratuletur quod ante vetustas non intellectum venerabatur. Eadem tamen quae didicisti doce, ut cum dicas nove, non dicas nova.

XXIII

S ED FORSITAN DICIT ALIQUIS: Nullusne ergo in Ecclesia Christi profectus habebitur Religionis?

Habeatur plane, et maximus. Nam quis ille est tam invidus hominibus, tam exosus Deo, qui istud prohibere conetur? Sed ita tamen ut vere profectus sit ille fidei, non permutatio. Siquidem ad profectum pertinet ut in semetipsum unaquaeque res amplificetur; ad permutationem vero, ut aliquid ex alio in aliud transvertatur. Crescat igitur oportet et multum vehementerque proficiat tam singulorum quam omnium, tam unius hominis quam totius Ecclesiae, aetatum ac saeculorum gradibus, intelligentia, scientia, sapientia, sed in suo dumtaxat: genere, in eodem scilicet dogmate, eodem sensu, eademque sententia.

Imitetur animarum religio rationem corporum: quae licet annorum processu numeros suos evolvant et explicent, eadem tamen quae erant permanent. Multum interest inter pueritiae florem et senectutis maturitatem; sed iidem

and knowledge, to be the Beseleel[57] of the spiritual Tab-
ernacle, to cut the precious gems of divine dogma, to put
them together faithfully, to adorn them judiciously, to add
glamor, grace, and loveliness, may that which was formerly
believed with difficulty be made, through your interpretation, more understandable in the light. May posterity,
through your aid, rejoice in the understanding of things
which in old times were venerated without understanding.
Yet, teach precisely what you have learned; do not say new
things even if you say them in a new manner.

23

AT THIS POINT, THE QUESTION MAY BE
asked: If this is right, then is no progress of religion
possible within the Church of Christ?

To be sure, there has to be progress, even exceedingly
great progress. For who is so grudging toward his fellow
men and so full of hatred toward God as to try to pro-
hibit it? But it must be progress in the proper sense of the
word, and not a change in faith. Progress means that each
thing grows within itself,[58] whereas change implies that
one thing is transformed into another. Hence, it must be
that understanding, knowledge, and wisdom grow and
advance mightily and strongly in individuals as well as in
the community, in a single person as well as in the Church
as a whole, and this gradually according to age and history.
But they must progress within their own limits, that is, in
accordance with the same dogma, the same meaning, and
the same judgment.

The growth of religion in the soul should be like the
growth of the body, which in the course of years develops
and unfolds, yet remains the same as it was. Much happens
between the prime of childhood and the maturity of old

---

[57] Beseleel was chosen by God above all others to construct the taber-
nacle, the Ark of the Covenant, and the sacred vessels (cf. Exod. 31:2ff.).
[58] The term *in semetipsum* seems to have supplanted adverbially the *in
idipsum* of the Vulgate version.

tamen ipsi fiunt senes qui fuerant adolescentes;
ut quamvis unius ejusdemque hominis status
habitusque mutetur, una tamen nihilominus
eademque natura, una eademque persona sit.
Parva lactentium membra, magna juvenum,
eadem ipsa sunt tamen. Quot parvulorum artus,
tot virorum; et si qua illa sunt quae aevi matu-
rioris aetate pariuntur, jam in seminis ratione
proserta sunt; ut nihil novum postea proferatur
in senibus quod non in pueris jam ante latitaverit.
Unde non dubium est hanc esse legitimam et
rectam proficiendi regulam, hunc ratum atque
pulcherrimum crescendi ordinem, si eas semper
in grandioribus partes ac formas numerus detexat
aetatis quas in parvulis Creatoris sapientia prae-
formaverat. Quod si humana species in aliquam
deinceps non sui generis vertatur effigiem, aut
certe addatur quippiam membrorum numero vel
detrahatur, necesse est ut totum corpus vel inter-
cidat, vel prodigiosum fiat, vel certe debilitetur:
ita etiam Christianae Religionis dogma sequatur
has decet profectuum leges, ut annis scilicet con-
solidetur, dilatetur tempore, sublimetur aetate,
incorruptum tamen illibatumque permaneat, et
universis partium suarum mensuris cunctisque
quasi membris ac sensibus propriis plenum atque
perfectum sit, quod nihil praeterea permutatio-
nis admittat, nulla proprietatis dispendia, nullam
definitionis sustineat varietatem.

Exempli gratia: Severunt majores nostri antiquitus in hac ecclesiastica segete triticeae fidei
semina: iniquum valde et incongruum est ut nos
eorum posteri pro germana veritate frumenti
subdititium zizaniae legamus errorem. Quin
potius hoc rectum et consequens est ut primis
atque extremis sibimet non discrepantibus, de
incrementis triticeae institutionis triticei quoque

age. But the old men of today, who were the adolescents of yesterday, although the figure and appearance of one and the same person have changed, are identical. There remains one and the same nature and one and the same person. The limbs of infants are small, those of young men large—yet they are the same. The joints of adult men are as many as those of young children; though some are developed only in maturity, they already existed virtually in the embryo. Hence, nothing new is later produced in old men that has not previously been latent in children. Therefore, without any doubt, this is the legitimate and correct rule of progress and the established and most impressive order of growth: the course of the years always completes in adults the parts and forms with which the wisdom of the Creator had previously imbued infants. If, on the other hand, the human form were turned into a shape of another kind, or if the number of members of the body were increased or decreased, then the whole body would necessarily perish, or become a monstrosity, or be in some way disabled. In the same way, the dogma of the Christian religion ought to follow these laws of progress, so that it may be consolidated in the course of years, developed in the sequence of time, and sublimated by age—yet remain incorrupt and unimpaired, complete and perfect in all the proportions of its parts and in all its essentials (let us call them members and senses), so that it does not allow of any change, or any loss of its specific character, or any variation of its inherent form.

To give an example. In ancient times, our forefathers sowed the seeds of the wheat of faith in that field which is the Church. It would be quite unjust and improper if we, their descendants, gathered, instead of the genuine truth of wheat, the false tares of error. On the contrary, it is logically correct that the beginning and the end be in agreement, that we reap from the planting of the wheat of doctrine the harvest of the wheat of dogma. In this

dogmatis frugem demetamus; ut cum aliquid ex illis seminum primordiis accessu temporis evolvatur, et nunc laetetur et excolatur, nihil tamen de germinis proprietate mutetur: addatur licet species, forma, distinctio, eadem tamen cujusque generis natura permaneat. Absit etenim ut rosea illa catholici sensus plantaria in carduos spinasque vertantur. Absit inquam, ut in isto spiritali paradiso de cinnamomi et balsami surculis lolium repente atque aconita proveniant. Quodcumque igitur in hac Ecclesia Dei agricultura fide patrum satum est, hoc idem filiorum industriâ decet excolatur et observetur, hoc idem floreat et maturescat, hoc idem proficiat et perficiatur. Fas est etenim ut prisca illa caelestis philosophiae dogmata processu temporis excurentur, limentur, poliantur; sed nefas est ut commutentur, nefas ut detruncentur, ut mutilentur. Accipiant, licet, evidentiam, lucem, distinctionem; sed retineant necesse est plenitudinem, integritatem, proprietatem.

Nam si semel admissa fuerit haec impiae fraudis licentia, horreo dicere quantum exscindendae atque abolendae Religionis periculum consequatur. Abdicata etenim qualibet parte catholici dogmatis, alia quoque atque item alia, ac deinceps alia et alia, jam quasi ex more et licito, abdicabuntur. Porro autem singillatim partibus repudiatis, quid aliud ad extremum sequetur, nisi ut totum pariter repudietur? sed e contra, si novitia veteribus, extranea domesticis, et profana sacratis admisceri coeperint, proserpat hic mos in universum necesse est ut nihil posthac apud Ecclesiam relinquatur intactum, nihil illibatum, nihil integrum, nihil immaculatum, sed sit ibidem deinceps impiorum ac turpium errorum lupanar ubi erat antea castae et incorruptae

way, none of the characteristics of the seed is changed, although something evolved in the course of time from those first seeds and has now expanded under careful cultivation. What may be added is merely appearance, beauty, and distinction, but the proper nature of each kind remains. May it never happen that the rose garden of the Catholic spirit be turned into a field of thistles and thorns. May it never happen that in this spiritual paradise darnel and poison ivy suddenly appear from growths of cinnamon and balsam. Whatever has been planted in the husbandry of God's Church by the faith of the fathers should, therefore, be cultivated and guarded by the zeal of their children; it should flourish and ripen; it should develop and become perfect. For it is right that those ancient dogmas of heavenly philosophy should in the course of time be thoroughly cared for, filed, and polished; but it is sinful to change them, sinful to behead them or mutilate them. They may take on more evidence, clarity, and distinctness, but it is absolutely necessary that they retain their plenitude, integrity, and basic character.

If such a license for impious fraud be granted only once, what terrible danger—I am afraid even to speak of it—would result, with religion being destroyed and abolished. If one tenet of Catholic dogma were renounced, another, then another, and finally one after the other would be abandoned, first by custom; and then as though by right. When one segment after the other had been rejected, what else would the final result be, except that the whole would be likewise rejected? On the other hand, once there is a beginning of mixing the new with the old, foreign ideas with genuine, and profane elements with sacred, this habit will creep in everywhere, without check. At the end, nothing in the Church will be left untouched, unimpaired, unhurt, and unstained. Where formerly there was the sanctuary of chaste and uncorrupted truth, there will be a brothel of impious and filthy errors. May divine

sacrarium veritatis. Sed avertat hoc a suorum mentibus nefas divina pietas, sitque hic potius impiorum furor.

Christi vero Ecclesia, sedula et cauta depositorum apud se dogmatum custos, nihil in his unquam permutat, nihil minuit, nihil addit, non amputat necessaria, non apponit superflua, non amittit sua, non usurpat aliena; sed omni industria hoc unum studet ut vetera fideliter sapienterque tractando, si qua sunt illa antiquitus informata et inchoata, accuret et poliat; si qua jam expressa et enucleata consolidet, firmet; si qua jam confirmata et definita, custodiat; denique quid unquam aliud Conciliorum decretis enisa est nisi ut quod antea simpliciter credebatur, hoc idem postea diligentius crederetur, quod antea lentius praedicabatur, hoc idem postea instantius praedicaretur, quod antea securius colebatur, hoc idem postea sollicitius excoleretur? Hoc, inquam semper, neque quicquam praeterea, Haereticorum novitatibus excitata, conciliorum suorum decretis catholica perfecit Ecclesia, nisi ut quod prius a Majoribus sola traditione susceperat, hoc deinde posteris etiam per Scripturae chirographum consignaret, magnam rerum summam paucis litteris comprehendendo, et plerumque, propter intelligentiae lucem, non novum fidei sensum novae appellationis proprietate signando.

XXIV

S ED AD APOSTOLUM REDEAMUS. *O Timothee*, inquit, *depositum custodi, devitans prophanas vocum novitates. Devita*, inquit, *quasi viperam, quasi scorpionem, quasi basiliscum, ne te non solum tactu, sed etiam visu afflatuque percutiant.* Quid est *devitare*? cum hujusmodi nec cibum

compassion divert such shocking impiety from the minds of its children; instead, may the impious crowd itself be left in its madness!

The Church of Christ, zealous and cautious guardian of the dogmas deposited with it, never changes any aspect of them. It does not diminish them or add to them; it neither trims what seems necessary nor grafts things superfluous; it neither gives up its own nor usurps what does not belong to it. But it devotes all its diligence to one aim: to treat tradition faithfully and wisely; to nurse and polish what from old times may have remained unshaped and unfinished; to consolidate and to strengthen what already was clear and plain; and to guard what already was confirmed and defined. After all, what have the councils brought forth in their decrees but that what before was believed plainly and simply might from now on be believed more diligently; that what before was preached rather unconcernedly might be preached from now on more eagerly; that what before was practiced with less concern might from now on be cultivated with more care? This, I say, and nothing but this, has the Catholic Church, aroused over the novelties of the heretics, again and again accomplished by the decrees of its councils, i.e., what it earlier received from our forefathers by tradition alone, it has handed down to posterity by authoritative decisions, condensing weighty matters in a few words, and particularly for the enlightenment of the mind, by presenting in new words the old interpretation of the faith.

24

BUT LET US RETURN TO THE APOSTLE. "O Timothy," he says, "keep that which is committed to thy trust, avoiding the profane novelties of words." "Avoiding" (1 Tim. 6:20), he says, as you would avoid a viper, a scorpion, or a basilisk, lest they strike you not only with their touch, but even with their look and breath. What does

sumere. Quid est, *devita*? *Si quis*, inquit, *venit ad vos, et hanc doctrinam non affert.* Quam *doctrinam*, nisi catholicam et universalem, et unam eamdemque per singulas aetatum successiones incorrupta veritatis traditione manentem, et usque in saecula sine fine mansuram? Quid tum? *Nolite*, inquit, *recipere eum in domum, nec ave ei dixeritis. Qui enim dicit illi ave, communicat operibus ejus malignis.*

Prophanas, inquit, *vocum novitates.* Quid est *prophanas*? Quae nihil habent sacri, nihil religiosi, ab Ecclesiae penetralibus, quae est templum Dei, penitus extraneas. Prophanas, inquit, vocum novitates. Vocum, id est, dogmatum, rerum, sententiarum novitates, quae sunt vetustati atque antiquitati contrariae: quae si recipiantur, necesse est ut fides beatorum patrum, aut tota, aut certe magnâ ex parte violetur; necesse est ut omnes omnium aetatum fideles, omnes sancti omnes casti, continentes, virgines, omnes clerici, levitae et sacerdotes, tanta confessorum millia, tanti martyrum exercitus, tanta urbium, tanta populorum celebritas et multitudo, tot insulae, provinciae, reges, gentes, regna, nationes, totus postremo jam paene terrarum orbis, per catholicam fidem Christo capiti incorporatus, tanto saeculorum tractu ignorasse, errasse, blasphemasse, nesciisse quid crederet, pronuntietur.

Prophanas, inquit, *vocum novitates devita*: quas recipere atque sectari nunquam Catholicorum, semper vero Haereticorum fuit. Et revera, quae unquam haeresis nisi sub certo nomine, certo loco, certo tempore ebullivit? Quis unquam haereses instituit nisi qui se prius ab Ecclesiae catholicae universitatis et antiquitatis consensione discreverit? Quod ita esse luce clarius exempla

"avoiding" mean? "With such a one, not so much as to eat" (1 Cor. 5:11). What does "avoiding" mean? "If any man come to you and bring not this doctrine" (2 John 10). Of course, this means the Catholic and universal doctrine, which remains one and the same through all successive ages in the uncorrupted tradition of truth, and which will remain so without end for ever and ever. What then? "Receive him not," St. John continues, "into the house, nor say to him, God speed you. For he that saith to him, God speed you, communicated with his wicked works" (2 John 10–11).

"Profane novelties of words," he says. What is "profane"? That which has nothing sacred, nothing religious, which is completely outside the inner sanctuary of the Church, God's Temple (1 Cor. 3:16). "Profane novelties of words," he says. "Of words," i.e., novelties of dogma, subject matter, and opinions, contrary to tradition and antiquity, which, should they be accepted, would of necessity defile the faith of the blessed fathers either entirely or to a great extent. If they are accepted, then it must be stated that all the faithful of all ages—all the saints, all the chaste and continent virgins, all the clerics, levites, and priests, the many thousands of confessors and the vast armies of martyrs, many cities and great masses of people, innumerable islands, provinces, kings, races, kingdoms, and nations, finally, almost the whole world, incorporated through the Catholic Church in Christ as Head—that all of them have for so many centuries been ignorant, have erred, have blasphemed, have not known what ought to be believed.

"Avoiding profane novelties of words," he says, novelties which were never accepted and followed by Catholics, but always by heretics. Indeed, when did a heresy ever boil up except under a definite name, at a definite place, and at a definite time? Who ever introduced a heresy who had not first separated from the common agreement prevailing in the universal and traditional Catholic Church? A few examples will support these statements by clearer

demonstrant. Quis enim unquam ante profanum illum Pelagium tantam virtutem liberi praesumpsit arbitrii ut ad hoc in bonis rebus per actus singulos adjuvandum necessariam Dei gratiam non putaret? Quis ante prodigiosum discipulum ejus caelestium reatu praevaricationis Adae omne humanum genus denegavit adstrictum? Quis ante sacrilegum Arium trinitatis unitatem discindere, quis ante sceleratum Sabellium unitatis Trinitatem confundere ausus est? Quis ante crudelissimum Novatianum crudelem Deum dixit, eo quod mallet mortem morientis quam ut revertatur et vivat? Quis ante magum Simonem, apostolica districtione percussum (a quo vetus ille turpitudinum gurges usque in novissimum Priscillianum continua et occulta successione manavit) auctorem malorum, id est, scelerum, impietatum, flagitiorumque nostrorum ausus est dicere creatorem Deum? Quippe quem adserit talem hominum manibus ipsam suis creare naturam, quae proprio quodam motu et necessariae cujusdam voluntatis impulsu nihil aliud possit, nihil aliud velit nisi peccare, eo quod furiis vitiorum omnium exagitata et inflammata in omnia turpitudinum barathra inexhausta cupiditate rapiatur.

Innumera sunt talia, quae brevitatis studio praetermittimus: quibus tamen cunctis satis evidenter perspicueque monstratur hoc apud omnes fere haereses quasi solemne esse ac legitimum, ut semper profanis novitatibus gaudeant,

evidence. Who, before the profane Pelagius, ever dared to attribute such power to free will as not to believe in the indispensable help of God's grace for our good deeds in every act? Who, before his monstrous[59] disciple, Celestius, denied that the entire human race was bound by the guilt of Adam's transgression? Who, before the sacrilegious Arius, was audacious enough to split the Unity of the Trinity, or, before the wicked Sabellius, to confuse the Trinity of the Unity? Who, before the most cruel Novatianus, called God cruel, on the ground that He preferred the death of a dying person to his conversion and life?[60] Who, before Simon Magus[61]—whom the Apostle's wrath had attacked[62] and from whom that old stream of disgrace has flown on in uninterrupted and secret succession down to the most recent heretic, Priscillian[63]—dared to say that God the Creator was the author of evil, that is, of our crimes, impieties, and infamies? He actually makes the statement that God with His own hand created such a nature in man that he, by his own initiative and by his entirely determined will, neither can do nor want to do anything but sin, because he is driven and inflamed by the furies of all the vices and dragged down by unquenchable lust into the abyss of depravity.

Innumerable are the examples we must omit, since we wish to be brief. But all of them make it sufficiently clear that the customary method of most heresies consists in rejoicing in "profane novelties," in loathing traditional

---

[59] Rauschen is not certain whether *prodigiosus* or *monstrosus* is here deservedly used by Vincent.

[60] Ezek. 33:11. The Novatians held that deadly sins, such as murder, fornication, and denying the faith, could not be remitted by the Church, but were reserved to God alone.

[61] St. Irenaeus (*Adv. haer:* 1.23.2f.) states of Simon the Samaritan that he taught that good works were unnecessary, and further, that by the commandments of God men were reduced to slavery.

[62] See Acts 8:20.

[63] Bishop of Gallaecia (now Galicia). This heresy had been founded on the teaching of the Manichaeans and the Gnostics.

antiquitatis scita fastidiant, et per oppositiones
falsi nominis scientiae a fide naufragent. Contra
vero Catholicorum hoc vere proprium, deposita
sanctorum patrum et commissa servare, dam-
nare profanas novitates, et sicut dixit atque iterum praedixit Apostolus, *si quis annuntiaverit
praeterquam quod acceptum est, anathema sit.*

XXV

H IC FORTASSE ALIQUIS INTER-
roget an et Haeretici divinae Scripturae
testimoniis utantur. Utuntur plane. et vehementer quidem. Nam videas eos volare per singula
quaeque sanctae legis volumina, per Moysi, per
Regum libros; per Psalmos, per Apostolos, per
Evangelia, per Prophetas. Sive enim apud suos,
sive alienos, sive privatim, sive publice, sive in
sermonibus, sive in libris, sive in conviviis, sive
in plateis, nihil unquam paene de suo proferunt
quod non etiam Scripturae verbis adumbrare
conentur. Lege Pauli Samosateni opuscula, Pri-
scilliani, Eunomii, Joviniani, reliquarumque
pestium; cernas infinitam exemplorum conge-
riem, prope nullam omitti paginam quae non
novi aut veteris Testamenti sententiis fucata et
colorata sit. Sed tanto magis cavendi et pertime-
scendi sunt, quanto occultius sub divinae legis
umbraculis latitant. Sciunt enim faetores suos
nulli fere cito esse placituros, si nudi et simplices
exhalentur; atque idcirco eos caelestis eloquii
velut quodam aromate aspergunt, ut ille qui
humanum facile despiceret errorem, divina non
facile contemnat oracula. Itaque faciunt quod hi
solent, qui parvulis austera quaedam temperaturi
pocula, prius oras melle circumlinunt, ut incauta
aetas cum dulcedinem praesenserit, amaritudi-
nem non reformidet. Quod etiam iis curae est

knowledge, which some rejecting have made shipwreck concerning the faith (1 Tim. 1:19; 6:20). Conversely, it is proper for Catholics to guard the "deposit" handed down by the holy fathers, to condemn profane novelties, and, as the Apostle said "before and now I say again," let him be anathema "if any one preach to you a gospel besides that which you have received" (Gal. 1:9).

25

AT THIS POINT ONE MAY ASK ME: DO the heretics also make use of the testimonies of Holy Scripture? Indeed they do; and to a great degree. They go through each and every book of the Bible: Moses and the Books of Kings, the Psalms, the Apostles, the Gospels, the Prophets. They utter almost nothing of their own that they do not try to support with passages from the Scripture— whether they are among their own disciples or among strangers, in private or in public, whether in sermons or in writings, in private meetings or in forums. Read the treatises of Paul of Samosata, of Priscillian, of Eunomius, of Jovinian,[64] and of the rest of these pests, and you will discover an abundance of examples; there is scarcely a page that is not painted and illumined with texts from the Old and New Testaments. One must be on guard and fear them all the more because they are concealed under the protective shade of divine Law. They know well that their putrid products would not easily please anyone if their vapors were emitted undisguised; therefore, they sprinkle them with the perfume of divine words, knowing too well that anyone who readily despises human errors would hesitate to set aside divine prophecies. Thus, they behave like those who have to prepare a bitter drink for their infants and first smear some honey around the rim of the cup so that the unsuspecting child may not be averse to the bitterness when he has first sipped the sweet taste,

---

[64] For the extant works of these heretics, cf. Rauschen, *Vincentii Lerinensis Commonitoria 54*, nos. 3ff.

qui mala gramina et noxios succos medicaminum vocabulis praecolorant, ut nemo fere ubi suprascriptum legerit remedium, suspicetur venenum.

Inde denique et Salvator clamabat: *Attendite vobis a pseudoprophetis, qui veniunt ad vos in vestitu ovium, ab intus autem sunt lupi rapaces.* Quid est vestitus ovium, nisi Prophetarum et Apostolorum proloquia, quae iidem, ovili quadam sinceritate, agno illi immaculato, qui tollit peccatum mundi, tamquam vellera quaedam texuerunt? Qui sunt *lupi rapaces*, nisi sensus Haereticorum feri et rabidi, qui caulas Ecclesiae semper infestant et gregem Christi quaqua possunt dilacerant? Sed ut fallacius incautis ovibus obrepant, manente luporum ferocia, deponunt lupinam speciem, et sese divinae legis sententiis velut quibusdam velleribus obvolvunt, ut cum quisque lanarum mollitiem praesenserit, nequaquam aculeos dentium pertimescat. Sed quid ait Salvator? *Ex fructibus eorum cognoscetis eos*: id est, cum coeperint divinas illas voces non jam proferre tantum, sed etiam exponere, nec adhuc jactare solum, sed etiam interpretari, tunc amaritudo illa, tunc acerbitas, tunc rabies intelligetur, tunc novitium virus exhalabitur, tunc profanae novitates aperientur; tunc primum scindi sepem videas, tunc transferri patrum terminos, tunc Catholicam fidem caedi, tunc Ecclesiasticum dogma lacerari.

Tales erant ii quos percutit Apostolus Paulus in secunda ad Corinthios Epistola, dicens: *Nam ejusmodi, inquit, pseudoapostoli, sunt operarii subdoli, transfigurantes se in Apostolos Christi?* Quid est *transfigurantes se in Apostolos Christi*? Proferebant Apostoli divinae legis exempla; proferebant et illi. Proferebant Apostoli psalmorum auctoritates;

or like those who take great pains to embellish poisonous herbs and noxious juices with high-sounding medical names, so that no one suspects the poison while reading the labels on the mixture.

After all, that is why the Saviour exclaimed: "Beware of false prophets, who come to you in the clothing of sheep, but inwardly they are ravening wolves" (Matt. 7:15). What does "the clothing of sheep" mean save the words of the Prophets and Apostles, which these men in their pretended lamblike simplicity put on as a fleece, imitating the lamb unspotted (1 Pet. 1:19) "who taketh away the sin of the world" (John 1:29)? What are "ravening wolves"? What but the fierce and insane doctrines of the heretics who invade the sheepfold of the Church, wherever they can, and harass the flock of Christ? To approach the trusting sheep more deceitfully, they discard their wolflike appearance, though keeping their wolfish ferocity, and cover themselves with quotations from the Bible as though these were fleece. Thus, no one who has first felt the softness of the wool will fear the sharpness of their teeth. How does the Saviour continue? "By their fruits you shall know them" (Matt. 7:16). This means: Once they begin not only to use the divine expressions but also to explain them, not only to present them but also to interpret them, then people will realize how bitter, how sharp, how fierce they are. Then will the poisonous breath of their new ideas be exhaled, then will "profane novelties" appear in the open, then will you see that "the hedge is broken" (Eccl. 10:8), that the ancient bounds have been passed (Prov. 22:28), that the dogma of the Church is lacerated, that the Catholic faith is harmed.

Such were those whom the Apostle Paul attacked in the Second Epistle to the Corinthians, when he says: "For they are false apostles, deceitful workmen, transforming themselves into the apostles of Christ" (2 Cor. 11:13). What does "transforming themselves into the apostles of Christ" mean? The Apostles quoted the divine Law; so did the heretics. The Apostles adduced the authority of the

proferebant et illi. Proferebant Apostoli sententias Prophetarum; et illi nihilominus proferebant.
Sed cum ea quae similiter protulerant, interpretari non similiter coepissent, tunc simplices
a subdolis, tunc infucati a fucatis, tunc recti a
perversis, tunc postremo veri Apostoli a falsis
Apostolis discernebantur. *Et non mirum*, inquit.
Ipse enim Satanas transfigurat se in angelum lucis.
Non est ergo magnum si ministri ejus transfi-
gurantur sicut ministri justitiae. Ergo secundum
Apostoli Pauli magisterium, quotiescumque vel
pseudoapostoli vel pseudoprophetae vel pseu-
dodoctores divinae legis sententias proferunt,
quibus male interpretatis errores suos adstruere
conentur, non dubium est quin auctoris sui cal-
lida machinamenta sectentur, quae ille nunquam
profecto comminisceretur, nisi sciret omnino
nullam esse ad fallendum faciliorem viam, quam
ut ubi nefarii erroris subinducitur fraudulentia,
ibi divinorum verborum praetendatur auctoritas.

XXVI

S ED DICET ALIQUIS: UNDE PRO-
batur quia sacrae legis exemplis Diabolus
uti soleat?

Legat Evangelia, in quibus scribitur: Tunc
assumpsit illum Diabolus, id est, Dominum
Salvatorem, et statuit illum super pinnam tem-
pli, et dixit ei: *Si filius Dei es, mitte te deorsum.*
Scriptum est enim quod angelis suis mandavit de
te ut custodiant te in omnibus viis tuis; in mani-
bus tollent te, ne forte offendas ad lapidem pedem
tuum. Quid hic faciet misellis hominibus qui
ipsum Dominum majestatis Scripturarum testimoniis appetivit? *Si*, inquit, *filius Dei es, mitte*

Psalms; so did they. The Apostles invoked texts from the Prophets; so did they. But, when they began to interpret in an inaccurate way what they had accurately quoted, it became easy to distinguish the simple-minded from the deceitful, the unsophisticated from the sophisticated, the upright from those of perverted mind; in short, the true apostles from the false. "And no wonder, for Satan himself transformeth himself into an angel of light. Therefore it is no great thing if his ministers be transformed as the ministers of justice" (2 Cor. 11:14–15). Hence, according to the teaching of the Apostle Paul, whenever false apostles, false prophets, or false doctors quote passages from the Bible — in an attempt to support their errors with the aid of wrong interpretations — they are obviously imitating the cunning machinations of their master.[65] Satan certainly would never have invented them if he had not known that there was no easier way to deceive people than by pretending to the authority of the Bible when wicked errors were to be fraudulently introduced.

26

SOME ONE MAY OFFER THE OBJECTION: Where is the proof that Satan is accustomed to make use of examples taken from the Bible?

Let him who asks such a question read the Gospel in which it is written: "Then the devil took him" (the Saviour, our Lord) "up into the holy city and set him upon the pinnacle of the Temple, and said to him, If thou be the Son of God, cast thyself down; for it is written, that He hath given His angels charge over thee; and in their hands they shall bear thee up, lest thou dash thy foot against a stone" (Matt. 4:5–6). What can he not do to wretched human beings — he who assailed the "Lord of Glory" (1 Cor. 2:8) Himself with quotations from the Bible? "If thou be the Son of God," he said, "cast thyself down." Why? "For it is

---

[65] Namely, the Devil.

te deorsum. Quare? *Scriptum est enim,* inquit. Magnopere nobis doctrina loci istius attendenda atque retinenda est, ut tanto evangelicae auctoritatis exemplo, quando aliquos apostolica seu prophetica verba proferre contra catholicam fidem viderimus, diabolum per eos loqui minime dubitemus. Nam sicut tunc caput capiti, ita nunc quoque membra membris loquuntur, membra scilicet diaboli membris Christi, perfidi fidelibus, sacrilegi religiosis, Haeretici postremo Catholicis. Sed quid tandem dicunt? *Si,* inquit, *filius Dei es, mitte te deorsum; hoc est, si filius esse vis Dei et haereditatem regni caelestis accipere, mitte te deorsum, id est, ex istius te sublimis Ecclesiae, quae etiam templum Dei putatur, doctrina et traditione demitte.* Ac si quis interroget quempiam haereticorum sibi talia persuadentem: *Unde probas, unde doces quod Ecclesiae Catholicae universalem et antiquam fidem dimittere debeam*? statim ille: *Scriptum est enim.* Et continuo mille testimonia, mille exempla, mille auctoritates parat de lege, de Psalmis, de Apostolis, de Prophetis, quibus novo et malo more interpretatis, ex arce catholica in haereseos barathrum infelix anima praecipitetur.

Jam vero illis quae sequuntur promissionibus miro modo incautos homines Haeretici decipere consueverunt. Audent etenim polliceri et docere quod in Ecclesia sua, id est, in communionis suae conventiculo, magna et specialis ac plane personalis quaedam sit Dei gratia, adeo ut sine ullo labore, sine ullo studio, sine ulla industria, etiamsi nec petant, nec quaerant, nec pulsent, quicumque illi ad numerum suum pertinent, tamen ita divinitus dispensentur ut angelicis evecti manibus, id est, angelica protectione servati, nunquam possint offendere ad lapidem pedem suum, id est, nunquam scandalizari.

written." We should give particular attention to the lesson to be drawn from this passage. In the face of such an outstanding example of evangelical authority, we should never doubt that, every time we see people offering texts of the Apostles and Prophets against the Catholic faith, Satan is speaking through them. For, just as at that time the head (of the devils) spoke to the head (of the Church-to-be), so now do members speak to members, namely, members of the Devil's body to members of Christ's Body, perfidious men to the faithful, sacrilegious ones to the religious; in short, heretics to Catholics. What do they say? "If thou be the Son of God, cast thyself down." This means: If you want to be a son of God and possess the inheritance of the heavenly kingdom, cast yourself down, that is, separate yourself from the doctrine and tradition of that sublime Church which is God's Temple. But if you ask one of the heretics who is about to persuade you to such ideas: "What are the foundations of your arguments and teachings, according to which I have to give up the universal and traditional faith of the Catholic Church?" he will immediately say: "For it is written." He will then present you with thousands of testimonies, examples, and authorities — from the Law, the Psalms, the Apostles, the Prophets — which in his new and wrong interpretation precipitate your unhappy soul from the Catholic fortress into the abyss of heresy.

Here are the promises by which the heretics usually mislead those who are wanting in foresight. They[66] dare to promise in their teaching that in *their* church — that is, in their own small circle, is to be found a great and special and entirely personal form of divine grace; that it is divinely administered, without any pain, zeal, or effort on their part, to all persons belonging to their group, even if they do not ask or seek or knock. Thus, borne up by angels' hands — that is, preserved by angelic protection, they can never "dash their foot against a stone," they can never be scandalized.

---

[66] The followers of Semi-Pelagianism (see Rauschen, *Vincentii Lerinensis Commonitoria* 56).

XXVII

S ED DICET ALIQUIS: SI DIVINIS eloquiis, sententiis, promissionibus et Diabolus et discipuli ejus utuntur, quorum alii sunt pseudoapostoli, alii pseudoprophetae et pseudomagistri, et omnes ex toto Haeretici, quid facient Catholici homines et matris Ecclesiae filii? Quonam modo in Scripturis sanctis veritatem a falsitate discernent? Hoc scilicet facere magnopere curabunt, quod in principio Commonitorii istius sanctos et doctos viros nobis tradidisse scripsimus, ut divinum Canonem secundum universalis Ecclesiae traditiones et juxta Catholici dogmatis regulas interpretentur; in qua item Catholica et apostolica Ecclesia sequantur necesse est universitatem, antiquitatem, consensionem. Et si quando pars contra universitatem, novitas contra vetustatem, unius vel paucorum errantium dissensio contra omnium vel certe multo plurium Catholicorum consensionem rebellaverit, praeferant partis corruptioni universitatis integritatem: in qua eadem universitate, novitatis profanitati antiquitatis religionem, itemque in ipsa vetustate, unius sive paucissimorum temeritati primum omnium generalia, si qua sunt, universalis Concilii decreta praeponant; tunc deinde, si id minus est, sequantur quod proximum est, multorum atque magnorum consentientes sibi sententias magistrorum. Quibus, adjuvante Domino, fideliter, sobrie, sollicite observatis, non magna difficultate noxios quosque exsurgentium Haereticorum deprehendemus errores.

XXVIII

H IC JAM CONSEQUENS ESSE video ut exemplis demonstrem quonam

27

WE NOW DEAL WITH THE FOLLOWING question: If it is true that Satan and his disciples, of whom some are false apostles, some, false prophets, and some, false teachers, but all entirely heretical, make use of Scriptural passages, texts, and promises—what should Catholics, children of Holy Mother Church, do? How shall they discern in Holy Scripture truth from falsehood? Here is the answer as we gave it at the beginning of this Commonitory,[67] in accordance with what holy and scholarly men have handed on to us. They will devote all their care and attention to interpreting the divine Canon according to the traditions of the Universal Church and the rules of Catholic dogma; within the Catholic and Apostolic Church they must follow the principles of universality, antiquity, and consent. If, at any time, a part is in rebellion against the whole, or some novelty against tradition, or if there is a dissension of one or a few involved in error against the consent of all or the vast majority of Catholics, then they should prefer the integrity of the whole to the corruption of a part. Further, within the same universality, they should place traditional religion before profane novelty. Likewise, within tradition, before the inconsiderate attitude of a very few they should place, first, the general decrees (if there are any) of a universal council, and, then, if this is less important, they should follow the concordant opinions of great and outstanding teachers. If, with God's help, these rules are cautiously and carefully observed, then we may with little difficulty control all the noxious errors of rebellious heretics.

28

FOLLOWING UP THE PRECEDING CON-siderations, I have now to show by examples how

---

[67] See ch. 2.

modo prophanae Haereticorum novitates prola-
tis atque collatis veterum magistrorum concor-
dantibus sibimet sententiis et deprehendantur et
condemnentur. Quae tamen antiqua sanctorum
patrum consensio non in omnibus divinae legis
quaestiunculis, sed solum certe praecipue in fidei
regula magno nobis studio et investiganda est et
sequenda. Sed neque semper neque omnes haereses hoc modo impugnandae sunt, sed novitiae
recentesque tantummodo, cum primum scilicet
exoriuntur, ante quam infalsare vetustae fidei
regulas ipsius temporis vetantur angustiis, ac pri-
usquam manante latius veneno, majorum volumina vitiare conentur. Ceterum dilatatae et inve-
teratae haereses nequaquam hac via adgrediendae
sunt, eo quod prolixo temporum tractu longa iis
fruendae veritatis patuerit occasio. Atque ideo
quascumque illas antiquiores vel schismatum vel
haereseon profanitates nullo modo nos oportet
nisi aut sola, si opus est, Scripturarum auctoritate
convincere, aut certe jam antiquitus universalibus
sacerdotum catholicorum Conciliis convictas
damnatasque vitare.

Itaque, cum primum mali cujusque erroris putredo erumpere coeperit, et ad defen-
sionem sui quaedam sacrae legis verba furari,
eaque fallaciter et fraudulenter exponere, statim interpretando Canoni majorum sententiae
congregandae sunt; quibus illud quodcumque
exsurget novitium, ideoque profanum et absque
ulla ambage prodatur, et sine ulla retractatione
damnetur. Sed eorum dumtaxat patrum sententiae conferendae sunt, qui in fide et communione Catholica sancte, sapienter, constanter
viventes, docentes, et permanentes, vel mori in
Christo fideliter vel occidi pro Christo feliciter
meruerunt. Quibus tamen hac lege credendum

the profane novelties of the heretics can be detected and condemned by quoting from, and collating with each other, the concordant opinions of the ancient teachers. However, we must carefully investigate and follow this traditional consent of the holy fathers, not in every minor problem concerning the divine Law, but certainly and particularly for the basis and for the rules of faith. Moreover, we need not always fight in this way against all heresies, but only against those which are new and recent; but, in the latter case, as soon as they appear, before they have time to falsify the rules of traditional faith, and before they spread their poison any farther to spoil what our forefathers have written. Inveterate and widespread heresies are in nowise to be attacked by this method, because in the course of their long histories they had ample opportunity to plagiarize the truth. Thus, those older abominations of schisms or heresies cannot be overcome save by refuting[68] them (if necessary) on the authority of Holy Scripture alone, or by avoiding them if they formerly have been refuted and condemned by universal councils of the Catholic bishops.

Therefore, as soon as the foulness of some evil error begins to break out and its defenders abuse passages of Holy Scripture and explain them deceitfully and fraudulently, the opinions of our ancestors must immediately be collected for the interpretation of the Canon. Each novelty, hence, each abomination that may arise will thus be brought to light without ambiguity and be condemned outright. But only those opinions of the fathers are to be brought forward which were expressed by those who lived, taught, and persevered in the holy Catholic faith and communion, and who deserved either to die faithfully in Christ or to be martyred gloriously for Him. Those men are to be believed, moreover, in accordance with the

---

[68] On this matter, Tertullian (*De praescr.* 19) disagreed.

est ut quicquid vel omnes vel plures uno eodemque sensu manifeste, frequenter, perseveranter,
velut quodam consentiente sibi magistrorum
concilio, accipiendo, tenendo, tradendo firma-
verint, id pro indubitato, certo, ratoque habeatur.
Quicquid vero, quamvis ille sanctus et doctus,
quamvis Confessor et Martyr, praeter omnes aut
etiam contra omnes senserit, id inter proprias
et occultas et privatas opiniunculas a communis
et publicae ac generalis sententiae auctoritate
secretum sit; ne cum summo aeternae salutis
periculo, juxta sacrilegam Haereticorum et Schi-
smaticorum consuetudinem, universalis dogmatis antiqua veritate dimissa, unius hominis
novitium sectemur errorem.

Quorum beatorum patrum sanctum catholi-
cumque consensum, ne quis sibi temere contem-
nendum forte arbitretur, ait in prima ad Corinthios Apostolus: *Et quosdam quidem posuit Deus in
Ecclesia primum Apostolos* (quorum ipse unus erat),
secundo Prophetas (qualem in Actibus Apostolorum
legimus Agabum), *tertio Doctores*, qui tractatores
nunc appellantur, quos hic idem Apostolus etiam
Prophetas interdum nuncupat, eo quod per eos
Prophetarum mysteria populis aperiantur. Hos
ergo in Ecclesia Dei divinitus per tempora et loca
dispensatos quisquis in sensu catholici dogmatis
unum aliquid in Christo sentientes contempserit,
non hominem contemnit, sed Deum: a quorum
veridica unitate ne discrepet, impensius obtesta-
tur idem Apostolus dicens: *Obsecro autem vos, fratres, ut id ipsum dicatis omnes, et non sint in vobis schi-
smata, sitis autem perfecti in eodem sensu et in eadem
sententia* (1 Cor. 1). Quod si quis ab eorum sententiae communione desciverit, audiet illud ejusdem
Apostoli: *Non est Deus dissensionis, sed pacis* (id est,
non ejus qui a consentiendi unitate defecerit, sed

following rule: only that is to be held as certain, valid and beyond doubt, which either all or most of them have confirmed in one and the same sense — manifestly, frequently, and persistently, as though a council of masters stood in agreement — and which they have accepted, kept, and handed on. On the other hand, what some saint, learned man, bishop, confessor, or martyr has individually thought outside of, or even contrary to, the general opinion, must be considered his personal, particular, and quite private opinion, entirely removed from the common, public, and general opinion. If we respect such a rule, we shall not fall into the sacrilegious custom of the heretics and schismatics, who reject the ancient truth of universal dogma and follow the error of one man, and we shall thus escape the very grave danger of losing our eternal salvation.

Lest anyone think that the holy and Catholic consent of those blessed fathers can arbitrarily be despised, the Apostle says in his First Epistle to the Corinthians: "And God indeed hath set some in the church, first apostles" (of whom he was one), "secondly prophets" (as Agabus, mentioned in the Acts), "thirdly doctors" (1 Cor. 12:28) (who are now called *"tractatores"* — interpreters, also called Prophets by the same Apostle because the mysteries of the Prophets were made plain by them to the people). Everyone, therefore, who disregards these men whom God has given to His Church in all times and in all places, who disregards them when they agree in Christ about the interpretation of Catholic dogma, does not disregard man, but God Himself. Lest anyone cease to adhere to their true unity, the same Apostle urgently implores him: "Now I beseech you, brethren . . . that you all speak the same thing; and that there be no schisms among you, but that you be perfect in the same mind and in the same judgment" (1 Cor. 1:10). But, if someone has departed from the general opinion, let him listen further to the same Apostle: "God is not the God of dissension, but of peace," i.e., not the God of men who revolt against the common consent, but

eorum qui in consentiendi pace permanserint) *sicut in omnibus,* inquit, *Ecclesiis sanctorum doceo,* id est, Catholicorum: quae ideo sanctae sunt, quia in fidei communione persistunt.

Et ne quis forsitan, praetermissis ceteris, se solum audiri, sibi soli credi adrogaret, paulo post ait. *An a vobis,* inquit, *verbum Dei processit, aut in vos solos devenit?* Et ne hoc quasi perfunctorie acciperetur, adjecit: *Si quis,* inquit, *videtur propheta esse aut spiritalis, cognoscat quae scribo vobis, quia Domini sunt mandata.* Quae utique mandata, nisi ut si quis est propheta aut spiritalis, id est, spiritalium rerum magister, summo studio aequalitatis et unitatis cultor existat; ut scilicet neque opiniones suas ceteris praeferat, et ab universorum sensibus non recedat. Cujus rei mandata qui ignorat, inquit, ignorabitur: id est, qui aut nescita non discit, aut scita contemnit, ignorabitur, hoc est, indignus habebitur qui inter unitos fide et exaequatos humilitate divinitus respiciatur: quo malo nescio an quicquam acerbius cogitari queat. Quod tamen juxta apostolicam comminationem Pelagiano illi provenisse cernimus Juliano, qui se collegarum sensui aut incorporare neglexit, aut excorporare praesumpsit.

Sed jam tempus est ut pollicitum proferamus exemplum, ubi et quomodo sanctorum patrum sententiae congregatae sint, ut secundum eas ex decreto atque auctoritate Concilii ecclesiasticae fidei regula figeretur. Quod quo commodius fiat, hic sit jam hujus Commonitorii modus; ut cetera quae sequuntur, ab alio sumamus exordio.

of those who maintain the peace of agreement, "as also I teach in all the churches of the saints" (1 Cor. 14:33). This further means: in the churches of Catholics, which are holy because they persevere in the communion of faith.

And lest anyone arrogantly claim that he alone should be heard and believed, all the rest being set aside, the Apostle continues a little later: "Or did the word of God come out from you? Or came it only unto you?" In order to be more emphatic, he adds: "If any seem to be a prophet or spiritual, let him know that the things that I write to you are the commandments of the Lord" (1 Cor. 14:36–37). What other commandments than that he who is "a prophet or spiritual" — a teacher of spiritual matter — cultivate to the utmost the principles of harmony and unity, and, therefore, never prefer his personal opinions to those of all the others or depart from the general opinion? If any man, the Apostle concludes, "know not" these commandments, "he shall not be known" (1 Cor. 14:38). This means that he who does not learn what he does not know, or who disregards what he does know, "shall not be known," that is, shall be considered unworthy to be counted by God among those who are united in faith and made equal by humility. Is there any greater disaster imaginable than that? But, in accordance with the Apostle's threat, precisely this occurred, as we saw only recently, to the Pelagian Julian,[69] who did not care to belong to the united body of his brethren, and had the self-conceit to exclude himself from that body.

But now it is time to present the example[70] I promised and to show where and how the opinions of the holy fathers have been collected so that, in accordance with them, the Church's rule of faith may be fixed by the decree and authority of a council. To accomplish my plan more conveniently, it is best to close this Commonitory here and to start anew on what I still have to say.

---

[69] Julian, Bishop of Eclanum, a city in Apulia, a man much skilled in Greek and Latin, and always ready for a fight, upheld the Pelagian heresy against St. Augustine, who answered him in the six books *Contra Julianum*.
[70] See the beginning of this chapter.

[*Secundum Commonitorium interlapsum est, neque ex eo amplius quicquam quam postrema particula remansit, id est, sola recapitulatio, quae et subjecta est.*]

XXIX

QUAE CUM ITA SINT, JAM TEM-pus est ut ea quae duobus his Commonito-riis dicta sunt, in hujus secundi fine recapitulemus.

Diximus in superioribus hanc fuisse semper et esse hodieque Catholicorum consuetudinem, ut fidem veram duobus his modis adprobent, pri-mum divini Canonis auctoritate, deinde Eccle-siae Catholicae traditione; non quia Canon solus non sibi ad universa sufficiat, sed quia verba divina pro suo plerique arbitratu interpretantes, varias opiniones erroresque concipiant, atque ideo necesse sit ut ad unam ecclesiastici sensus regulam Scripturae caelestis intelligentia diri-gatur, in his dumtaxat praecipue quaestionibus quibus totius Catholici dogmatis fundamenta nituntur. Item diximus in ipsa rursus Ecclesia universitatis pariter et antiquitatis consensionem spectari oportere; ne aut ab unitatis integritate in partem schismatis abrumpamur, aut a vetustatis religione in haereseon novitates praecipitemur.

Item diximus in ipsa Ecclesiae vetustate duo quaedam vehementer studioseque observanda, quibus penitus inhaerere deberent quicumque haeretici esse nollent: primum, si quid esset

*[The second Commonitory has been
lost. There remains of it nothing more
than the final fragment. That is, only the
recapitulation, which is here appended.]*[71]

29

THE TIME HAS COME TO RECAPITULATE here, at the end of the Second Commonitory, the content of both.

As we said in earlier sections, it always was, and is today, the usual practice of Catholics to test the true faith by two methods: first, by the authority of the divine Canon, and then, by the tradition of the Catholic Church.[72] Not that the Canon is insufficient in itself in each case. But, because most [false] interpreters of the Divine Word make use of their own arbitrary judgment and thus fall into various opinions and errors, the understanding of Holy Scripture must conform to the single rule of Catholic teaching — and this especially in regard to those questions upon which the foundations of all Catholic dogma are laid. We also said that within the Church itself an agreement of universality and antiquity must be observed, lest we are either drawn away from integral unity into the separatism of schism or precipitated from traditional belief into the novelties of heresy.

Moreover, we said that, with regard to the tradition of the Church, two precautions had to be rigorously and thoroughly observed, adhered to by everyone who does not wish to become a heretic: first, it must be ascertained

---

[71] These words, which are found in all the codices and early editions, cannot be those of Vincent. In regard to the second *Commonitory*, Gennadius (*De vir. ill.* 64) states: "Since, by theft, he lost the major portion of his work, written on scrolls, having briefly recapitulated the meaning, he first assembled, and then produced it in one volume."

[72] Origen, Irenaeus, and Tertullian agree with Vincent that, in deciding questions concerning the faith, tradition is reasonably to be adhered to. See, especially, the preface of Origen, *De principiis*.

antiquitus ab omnibus Ecclesiae Catholicae sacerdotibus universalis Concilii auctoritate decretum; deinde si qua nova exsurgeret quaestio, ubi id minime reperiretur, recurrendum ad sanctorum patrum sententias, eorum dumtaxat qui suis quisque temporibus et locis in unitate communionis et fidei permanentes, magistri probabiles exstitissent, et quicquid uno sensu atque consensu tenuisse invenirentur, id Ecclesiae verum et catholicum absque ullo scrupulo judicaretur.

Quod ne praesumptione magis nostra quam auctoritate ecclesiastica promere videremur, exemplum adhibuimus sancti Concilii quod ante triennium, ferme in Asia apud Ephesum celebratum est Basso Antiochoque Consulibus: ubi cum de sanciendis fidei regulis disceptaretur, ne qua illic forsitan profana novitas in modum perfidiae Ariminensis obreperet, universis sacerdotibus, qui illo ducenti fere numero convenerant, hoc catholicissimum, fidelissimum, atque optimum factu visum est ut in medium sanctorum patrum sententiae proferrentur, quorum alios martyres, alios confessores, omnes vero catholicos sacerdotes fuisse et permansisse constaret; ut scilicet rite atque solemniter ex eorum consensu atque decreto antiqui dogmatis religio confirmaretur

whether there exists from ancient times a decree established by all the bishops of the Catholic Church with
the authority of a universal council, and second, should
a new question arise for which no decree can be found,
one must revert to the opinions of the holy fathers; to be
more precise, of those fathers who remained in their own
times and places in the unity of communion and of faith
and who were therefore held as teaching "probable" doctrine. If we can discover what they held in full agreement
and consent, then we can conclude without hesitation
that this is the true and Catholic doctrine of the Church.

Since we sought to avoid the impression that we set
forth these principles more by our own presumption than
by the authority of the Church, we chose the example
of that holy council which took place about three years
ago at Ephesus in Asia, while the illustrious Bassus and
Antiochus[73] were consuls. When a debate arose on what
rules of faith should be sanctioned in order to avoid new
and profane novelties from creeping in as if by chance, as
had happened disastrously at the Council of Rimini,[74] the
nearly two hundred members[75] of the hierarchy who were
present declared the following procedure to be the most
Catholic and truly the best in the interests of the faith. [It
was agreed] by the assembled bishops that there should be
presented the opinions of the holy fathers, some of whom
were martyrs, others confessors, but all of them Catholic
bishops[76] who, as was well known, had remained so; and
that what they had unanimously accepted should be duly

---

[73] The year 431.

[74] At Rimini in 359, about four hundred bishops, "some overcome by
weakness of intellect, some worn out by traveling" (Sulpicius Severus,
Chron. 2.43), subscribed to a formula which decreed that the Son was
like (*hómoion*) to the Father.

[75] At the first session of the Council of Ephesus, held on June 22, one
hundred ninety-eight bishops, joined a short time later by some others,
deposed Nestorius. Prosper (*Chron. ad annum* 431) states as follows: "At
the synod of more than two hundred bishops, convened at Ephesus,
Nestorius was condemned, as was the heresy bearing his name; so also
were many Pelagians who were supporting very similar doctrines."

[76] *episcopoi* (in the text, *sacerdotes*).

et prophanae novitatis blasphemia condemnaretur. Quod cum ita factum foret, jure meritoque impius ille Nestorius catholicae vetustati
contrarius, beatus vero Cyrillus sacrosanctae
antiquitati consentaneus judicatus est. Et ut
ad fidem rerum nihil deesset, tam nomina
et numerum (licet ordinem fuissemus obliti)
edidimus eorum patrum juxta quorum ibidem
concinentem sibi concordemque sententiam et
legis sacrae proloquia exposita sunt, et divini
dogmatis regula constabilita est: quos, ad con-
firmandam memoriam, hic quoque recensere
nequaquam superfluum est.

XXX

S UNT ERGO HI VIRI QUORUM IN
illo Concilio vel tamquam judicum vel
tamquam testium scripta recitata sunt. Sanctus
Petrus Alexandrinus Episcopus doctor praestan-
tissimus et martyr beatissimus. Sanctus Athanasius, ejusdem civitatis antistes, magister fide-
lissimus et confessor eminentissimus. Sanctus
Theophilus, ejusdem item urbis Episcopus, vir
fide, vita, scientia satis clarus, cui successit venerandus Cyrillus, qui nunc Alexandrinam illustrat
Ecclesiam. Et ne forsitan unius civitatis ac provinciae doctrina haec putaretur, adhibita sunt
etiam illa Cappadociae lumina, Sanctus Gregorius Episcopus et confessor de Nazianzo; Sanctus
Basilius, Caesareae Cappadociae Episcopus et
confessor; Sanctus item alter Gregorius Nyssenus
Episcopus, fidei, conversationis, integritatis et
sapientiae merito, fratre Basilio dignissimus. Sed
ne sola Graecia aut Oriens tantum, verum etiam
Occidentalis et Latinus orbis ita semper sensisse
adprobaretur, lectae sunt quoque ibi quaedam

and solemnly confirmed as the dogma of the ancient faith, and thus, vice versa, the blasphemy of profane novelty condemned. They actually proceeded in this way. The impious Nestorius was formally and correctly judged as opposing ancient Catholic belief, while, on the other hand, blessed Cyril was declared to be in agreement with that most sacred tradition. Moreover, to make our report on the facts fully trustworthy, we also indicated the names and number—we had forgotten their rank—of those fathers according to whose unanimous and concordant opinion the words of the divine Law were explained and the rule of divine dogma established. To refresh our memory, it is worthwhile to recall their names here once more.

30

THESE ARE THE MEN WHOSE WRITINGS were quoted at that council, either as judges or as witnesses: St. Peter, Bishop of Alexandria, an outstanding doctor and most blessed martyr;[77] St. Athanasius, Bishop of that same city, a most faithful teacher and most eminent confessor; and St. Theophilus,[78] also Bishop of that city, a man famous for his faith, knowledge, and whole life, whose successor is the venerable Cyril, now an honor to the Church in Alexandria. But it would be wrong to conclude that this doctrine came only from one city and province. There were, in addition, those stars of Cappadocia: St. Gregory of Nazianzus, bishop and confessor; St. Basil, confessor and Bishop of Caesarea in Cappadocia; and that other Gregory, Bishop of Nyssa, who, through the merits of his faith, integrity, wisdom, and manner of life, was of equal worth with his brother Basil. Furthermore, to prove that the Western and Latin world, no less than Greece and the East, had always been in agreement, letters addressed

---

[77] Peter was Bishop of Alexandria from the year 300, and suffered martyrdom in 311 (see Eusebius, *Hist. eccl.* 9.6.2).
[78] Theophilus, Bishop of Alexandria, 385–412, was an opponent of St. John Chrysostom.

ad quosdam Epistolae sancti Felicis martyris
et sancti Julii, urbis Romae Episcoporum. Et
ut non solum caput orbis, verum etiam latera
illi judicio testimonium perhiberent, adhibitus
est a Meridie beatissimus *Cyprianus* Episcopus
Carthaginensis et martyr; a Septentrione sanctus
Ambrosius Mediolanensis Episcopus.

Hi sunt igitur omnes apud Ephesum sacrato
Decalogi numero magistri, consiliarii, testes,
judicesque producti; quorum beata illa Synodus
doctrinam tenens, consilium sequens, credens
testimonio, obediens judicio, absque taedio,
praesumptione, et gratia de fidei regulis pro-
nuntiavit. Quamquam multo amplior majorum
numerus adhiberi potuerit, sed necesse non fuit;
quia neque multitudine testium negotii tempora
occupari oportebat, et decem illos non aliud
vere sensisse quam ceteros omnes collegas suos
nemo dubitabat.

XXXI

POST QUAE OMNIA, ADJECIMUS
etiam beati Cyrilli sententiam, quae gestis
ipsis ecclesiasticis continetur. Namque cum lecta
esset Sancti Capreoli, Episcopi Carthaginensis
Epistola, qui nihil aliud intendebat et precabatur
nisi ut, expugnata novitate, antiquitas defen-
deretur, ita Episcopus Cyrillus prolocutus est
et definivit. Quod hic quoque interponere non
abs re videtur. Ait enim in fine gestorum: *Et haec,
inquit, quae lecta est Epistola venerandi et multum
religiosi Episcopi Carthaginensis Capreoli, fidei gestorum inseretur; cujus aperta sententia est. Vult etenim*

to various persons were read at that council, letters written
by St. Felix the Martyr and St. Julius,[79] both Bishops of the
city of Rome. And since witnesses should come not only
from the center, but also from the outposts of the world,
the meeting was also joined by the most blessed Cyprian,
Bishop of Carthage and martyr, from the South, and by
St. Ambrose, Bishop of Milan, from the North.

All these men, of a number[80] made sacred by the Dec-
alogue, were brought before the assembly at Ephesus as
teachers, counselors, witnesses, and judges, and that holy
council clung fast to their teaching, followed their advice,
believed in their testimony, obeyed their judgment, and
thus decided upon the rule of faith without any precon-
ceived prejudice or favor. To be sure, a far greater number
of fathers could have been added to this list, but there
was no need. Too many witnesses would have prolonged
unnecessarily the time of the debate; besides, no one had
the least doubt that the opinions of these ten men were,
by and large, identical with those of all their colleagues.

31

AFTER WE HAD RELATED ALL THESE
facts, we specifically quoted a sentence from blessed
Cyril which is included in the council's record. When the
letter of St. Capreolus,[81] Bishop of Carthage, had been
read—and he intended no more than to request that novelty be destroyed and tradition defended—Bishop Cyril
spoke, and concluded with a remark which it is apposite
to quote once more: "This letter of the venerable and most
pious Bishop of Carthage, Capreolus, which was just read
to us, may be introduced into the record. Its meaning is

---

[79] Felix I was Bishop of Rome, 269–274; Julius I, 337–352.
[80] Vincent forgot not only the rank, as he himself admits (ch. 29), but
also the number. For besides the ten whom he mentions, two others
are brought forward as witnesses to the truth: Atticus, who succeeded
St. Chrysostom at Constantinople, and Amphilochius, Bishop of Iconium (d. about 394).
[81] Capreolus succeeded Aurelius in the See of Carthage. This letter is
extant in both Greek and Latin (see Migne, *PL* 53:843ff.).

antiquae fidei dogmata confirmari, novitia vero et superflue adinventa et impie promulgata, reprobari atque damnari. Omnes Episcopi acclamaverunt: *Hae omnium voces sunt, haec omnes dicimus, hoc omnium votum est.* Quae tandem omnium voces, aut quae omnium vota, nisi ut quod erat antiquitus traditum teneretur, quod adinventum nuper, exploderetur?

Post quae admirati sumus et praedicavimus quanta Concilii illius fuerit humilitas et sanctitas, ut tot numero sacerdotes, paene ex majori parte Metropolitani, tantae eruditionis tantaeque doctrinae ut prope omnes possent de dogmatibus disputare, quibus propterea ipsa in unum congregatio audendi ab se aliquid et statuendi addere videretur fiduciam, nihil tamen novarent, nihil praesumerent, nihil sibi penitus adrogarent, sed omnimodis praecaverent ne aliquid posteris traderent quod ipsi a patribus non accepissent, et non solum in praesenti rem bene disponerent, verum etiam post futuris exempla praeberent ut et ipsi scilicet sacratae vetustatis dogmata colerent, profanae vero novitatis adinventa damnarent.

Invecti etiam sumus in Nestorii sceleratam praesumptionem, quod sacram Scripturam se primum et solum intelligere, et omnes eos ignorasse jactaret, quicumque ante se, magisterii munere praediti, divina eloquia tractavissent, universos scilicet sacerdotes, universos confessores et martyres, quorum alii explanassent Dei legem, alii vero explanantibus consensissent vel credidissent, totam postremo etiam nunc errare et semper errasse adseveraret Ecclesiam, quae, ut ipsi videbatur, ignaros erroneosque doctores et secuta esset et sequeretur.

obvious: he wishes that the dogma of traditional faith be confirmed and that the novelties—useless inventions as they are, propagated by impious hangers-on, be disapproved and condemned." All the bishops acclaimed, and cried: "These are the words of us all; this is what we all mean; this is what all of us desire."[82] To what purpose, this unanimous voice and vote? That the ancient tradition ought to be adhered to, and recent novelties rejected.

After that, we emphatically expressed our admiration for the great humility and sanctity of that council. There were assembled so many members of the hierarchy—almost all Metropolitans—of such high attainments in scholarship and doctrinal knowledge, that almost all of them were qualified to participate in discussions on dogmatic problems. Yet, although their meeting obviously might have tempted them to take the initiative in setting up additional rules of their own, they invented nothing new, they conjectured nothing, they claimed no privilege for themselves. On the contrary, they cared for only one thing: that they should by no means hand on to posterity anything which they themselves had not received from the fathers. In this way they not only settled effectively the problems with which they were faced at that time, but also set an example for future generations. These, too, should honor the doctrines of sacred tradition and condemn the fancies of profane novelty.

We also assailed the vicious presumption of Nestorius, who had boasted that he was the first and only one to understand the Scriptures and that all the others who had interpreted the divine Word before him were ignorant, even though they were truly gifted teachers—all the priests, confessors, and martyrs, some of whom had explained the divine Law, while others accepted or believed in their explanations. He even asserted that the entire Church was now involved in error and always had been so, because it had, in his opinion, followed and still was following ignorant and misguided doctors.

---

[82] Cf. Harduinus, *Acta conciliorum* 1.1.1422.

XXXII

QUAE OMNIA LICET CUMULATE abundeque sufficerent ad *profanas quasque novitates* obruendas et exstinguendas, tamen ne quid deesse tantae plenitudini videretur, ad extremum adjecimus geminam Apostolicae Sedis auctoritatem, unam scilicet sancti Papae Sixti qui nunc Romanam Ecclesiam venerandus illustrat, alteram decessoris sui beatae memoriae Papae caelestini, quam hic quoque interponere necessarium judicavimus.

Ait itaque sanctus Papa Xystus in Epistola quam de causa Nestorii Antiocheno misit Episcopo: *Ergo,* inquit, *quia, sicut ait Apostolus, fides una est, quae evidenter obtinuit, dicenda credamus et tenenda dicamus. Quae sunt tandem illa credenda et dicenda?* Sequitur, et ait: *Nihil ultra,* inquit, *liceat novitati, quia nihil addi convenit vetustati. Perspicua majorum fides et credulitas nulla coeni permixtione turbetur.* Omnino apostolice: ut majorum credulitatem perspicuitatis lumine ornaret, novitias vero profanitates caeni permixtione describeret. Sed et sanctus Papa caelestinus pari modo eademque sententia. Ait enim in Epistola quam Gallorum sacerdotibus misit, arguens eorum conniventiam quod antiquam fidem silentio destituentes, profanas novitates exsurgere paterentur: *Merito,* inquit, *causa nos respicit, si silentio foveamus errorem. Ergo corripiantur hujusmodi; non sit his liberum habere pro voluntate sermonem.* Hic aliquis fortasse addubitet quinam sint illi quos habere prohibeat

32

A LL THIS MATERIAL THAT WE HAVE accumulated should be more than sufficient to crush and eliminate every kind of "profane novelty." Yet, to make the evidence more complete, we still referred at the close—in addition to all other testimony—to two utterances made by authority of the Holy See: one by the holy Pope Sixtus III, that venerable man who at present does honor to the Roman Church; the other by his predecessor of happy memory, Pope Celestine I. We consider it necessary to repeat them here.

The holy Pope Sixtus said in a letter[83] which he sent to the Bishop of Antioch in the Nestorian affair: "Hence, because, as the Apostle said, there is 'one Faith' (Eph. 4:5) which he victoriously kept, let us believe in the things to be said, and speak the things to be maintained." But which are the things to be believed in and to be taught? The Pope continues: "Let no further advance of novelty be permitted, because it is unbecoming to add anything to ancient tradition; the transparent faith and belief of our forefathers should not be soiled by contact with dirt." It is truly apostolic to compare the riches of belief that our ancestors possessed to the transparency of light and to describe profane novelties as a mixture of dirt. The holy Pope Celestine wrote in the same manner and the same spirit. In a letter which he addressed to the bishops of Gaul and in which he accused them of passive collaboration, because by their silence they were forsaking the old faith and permitting "profane novelties" to arise, he said: "Rightly we have to bear the responsibility, if by our silence we encourage error. Therefore, those who behave in this way should be rebuked! They should have no right to free speech."[84] One may perhaps doubt whether those

---

[83] This letter, the sixth in the letters of Pope Sixtus III, was sent in 433 to John of Antioch, after the latter, who had previously favored Nestorius, had made his peace with St. Cyril (Migne, *PL* 50:609).

[84] *PL* 50:528.

liberum pro voluntate sermonem, vetustatis praedicatores, an novitatis adinventores. Ipse dicat, dubitationem legentium ipse dissolvat. Sequitur enim: *Desinat, inquit, si ita res est (id est, si ita est ut apud me quidam urbes et provincias vestras criminantur, quod eas quibusdam novitatibus consentire noxia dissimulatione faciatis), desinat itaque, inquit, si ita res est, incessere novitas vetustatem.* Ergo haec fuit beati caelestini beata sententia, ut non vetustas cessaret obruere novitatem, sed potius novitas desineret incessere vetustatem.

XXXIII

QUIBUS APOSTOLICISQUE catholicis decretis quisquis refragatur, insultet primum omnium necesse est memoriae sancti caelestini, qui statuit ut desineret incessere novitas vetustatem, deinde irrideat definita sancti Xysti, qui censuit ne ultra quicquam liceat novitati, quia nihil addi convenit vetustati, sed et beati Cyrilli statuta contemnat, qui venerandi Capreoli zelum magna praedicatione laudavit quod antiqua fidei dogmata confirmari cuperet, novitia vero adinventa damnari, Ephesinam quoque synodum, id est, totius paene Orientis sanctorum Episcoporum judicata proculcet, quibus divinitus placuit nihil aliud posteris credendum decernere nisi quod sacrata sibique in Christo consentiens sanctorum patrum tenuisset antiquitas, quique etiam vociferantes et adclamantes, uno ore testificati sunt has esse omnium voces, hoc omnes optare, hoc omnes censere; ut sicut universi fere ante Nestorium haeretici, contemnentes vetustatem, et adserentes novitatem, damnati fuissent, ita ipse quoque Nestorius, auctor novitatis, et

whom he wishes to deprive of the right to "free speech" are the preachers who have remained in keeping with tradition or the inventors of novelties. He himself answers this objection and dissipates such doubts, for he continues: "If that be so"—and he means: If it be true, as some men complain to me, that in your cities and provinces you encourage them by your harmful dissimulation to consent to some of those novelties—"if it be so," he says, "then stop such novelties from assailing tradition!" Thus, it was the sound opinion of blessed Celestine not that tradition should cease to crush novelties, but, on the contrary, that novelties should refrain from attacking tradition.

33

EVERYONE WHO IS OPPOSED TO THESE apostolic and Catholic decrees first deliberately insults the memory of St. Celestine, who made the point that novelties should cease from attacking tradition; secondly, derides the definitions of St. Sixtus, who was of the opinion that "no further advance should be permitted to novelties, because it is unbecoming to add anything to the ancient tradition"; and lastly, disregards the statements of St. Cyril, who in a fine sermon praised the zeal of the venerable Capreolus, because the latter desired that the "dogmas of the traditional faith be confirmed and that novel inventions be condemned." Further, such an opponent also rejects the Synod of Ephesus, that is, the judgments of the bishops of almost the entire East, whom it pleased under divine inspiration to decree that posterity should believe only what the sacred tradition, represented by the holy fathers, had unanimously maintained in Christ—the same synod whose members by unanimous vote attested that all of them agreed, with regard to wording, intention, and conviction, on the following decision: precisely as almost every heretic before Nestorius who disregarded tradition and adhered to novelty was condemned, so Nestorius himself, as the author of novelties and the assailant of tradition, should

impugnator vetustatis, condemnaretur. Quorum sacrosanctae et caelestis gratiae munere inspirata consensio si cui displicet, quid aliud sequitur, nisi ut profanitatem Nestorii adserat non jure damnatam? Ad extremum quoque universam Christi Ecclesiam et magistros ejus Apostolos et prophetas, praecipueque tamen beatum Apostolum Paulum, velut quaedam purgamenta contemnat; illam, quod a Religione colendae et excolendae semel sibi traditae fidei nunquam recesserit; illum vero, qui scripserit: *O Timothee, depositum custodi, devitans profanas vocum novitates,* et item: *Siquis vobis annuntiaverit praeterquam quod accepistis, anathema sit.*

Quod si neque apostolica definita neque ecclesiastica decreta temeranda sunt, quibus secundum sacrosanctam universitatis et antiquitatis consensionem cuncti semper haeretici, et ad extremum Pelagius, caelestius, Nestorius, jure meritoque damnati sunt, necesse est profecto omnibus deinceps Catholicis, qui sese Ecclesiae matris legitimos filios probare student, ut sanctae sanctorum Patrum fidei inhaereant, adglutinentur, immoriantur, profanas vero profanorum novitates detestentur, horrescant, insectentur, persequantur.

Haec sunt fere quae duobus Commonitoriis latius disserta, aliquanto nunc brevius recapitulandi lege constricta sunt; ut memoria mea, cui adminiculandae ista confecimus, et commonendi assiduitate reparetur, et prolixitatis fastidio non obruatur.

be condemned. If this sacred consent inspired by the gift of heavenly grace should displease anyone, what conclusion follows, save that, in the opinion of such persons, the condemnation of Nestorius' blasphemy was unjust? Finally, they can have nothing but disregard for the entire Church of Christ, for its teachers, apostles, and prophets, and above all for the blessed Apostle Paul, as though all of these were despicable; contempt for the Church, since it has never abandoned its awe-inspired respect for the faith that was once and for all handed over to it and that it has ever practiced and revered. It is also contempt for the Apostle, who wrote: "O Timothy, keep that which is committed to thy trust, avoiding the profane novelties of words" (1 Tim. 6:20), and again: "If anyone preach to you a gospel besides that which you have received, let him be anathema" (Gal. 1:9).

Therefore, it is not lawful to despise the apostolic definitions and ecclesiastical decrees, in which, in accordance with the sacred common consent and tradition, all heretics always have been justly condemned (as, of late, Pelagius, Celestius, and Nestorius were). It is, therefore, an indispensable obligation for all Catholics who are eager to prove that they are true sons of Holy Mother Church to adhere to the holy faith of the holy fathers, to preserve it, to die for it, and, on the other hand, to detest the profane novelties of profane men, to dread them, to harass and attack them.

This is more or less the subject matter which I discussed somewhat briefly in the two Commonitories, and a condensation of which I presented just now in the form of a recapitulation, in order to refresh my memory for the support of which I wrote this book by persistent recollection, without, however, overburdening it by unpleasant prolixity.

THE VINCENTIAN CANON AND UNANIMOUS CONSENT OF THE FATHERS

Phillip Campbell

I N THE MID-SEVENTEENTH CENTURY English Protestant divine William Chillingworth derided the concept of an unbroken apostolic tradition. In his book *Religion of the Protestants*, Chillingworth asserted that "There have been popes against popes: councils against councils: councils confirmed by popes against councils confirmed by popes: lastly the church of some ages against the church of other ages."[1] This assertion attempts to negate the force of the Catholic argument that Protestantism is not a fitting expression of Christian unity, since Protestant sects contradict each other. Chillingworth argued that the Catholic "unanimous consent of the fathers" is a mere illusion, a dream of Catholic apologists. It was Chillingworth's argument in part that prompted Cardinal Newman to write his famous *Essay on the Development of Christian Doctrine*. Newman, like many Catholic apologists, responded to this attack by referring to the principles of the Vincentian Canon.

In a certain sense, Newman's *Essay* is nothing other than an elaboration of the principles of the Vincentian Canon. Most traditional Catholics are familiar with the famous Vincentian Canon, named after St. Vincent of Lérins (d. 445). The canon is a threefold test to assess the orthodoxy of an idea, stating that only those things can be considered part of the Catholic deposit of faith which have been believed "everywhere, always, by all." The famed passage is found in Chapter 2 of his work the

---

[1] Thomas Birch, *The Works of W. Chillingworth* (Princeton University, 1840), 194.

Commonitorium. Let us begin by examining the passage in context. Having begun by affirming the authority of the Sacred Scripture, St. Vincent goes on to explain why the Bible alone is not a sufficient guide to faith:

> But here someone perhaps will ask: Since the canon of Scripture is complete, and sufficient of itself for everything, and more than sufficient, what need is there to join with it the authority of the Church's interpretation? For this reason — because, owing to the depth of Holy Scripture, all do not accept it in one and the same sense, but one understands its words in one way, another in another; so that it seems to be capable of as many interpretations as there are interpreters. For Novatian expounds it one way, Sabellius another, Donatus another, Arius, Eunomius, Macedonius, another, Photinus, Apollinaris, Priscillian, another, Iovinian, Pelagius, Celestius, another, lastly, Nestorius another. Therefore, it is very necessary, on account of so great intricacies of such various error, that the rule for the right understanding of the prophets and apostles should be framed in accordance with the standard of ecclesiastical and Catholic interpretation. (*Commonitorium*, 2)

Therefore Scripture cannot stand alone; it needs the "standard of ecclesiastical and Catholic interpretation" to ensure it is being understood aright.

But does this not involve us in a further difficulty of the same nature? If we need the Church's tradition to rightly interpret the Scripture, how do we know we are rightly interpreting the tradition? In other words, after admitting the necessity of a "standard of ecclesiastical and Catholic interpretation," how do we determine what that authentic standard is?

Taking up this objection, St. Vincent introduces his famous dictum:

In the Catholic Church itself, all possible care must be taken that we hold that faith which has been believed everywhere, always, by all. For that is truly and in the strictest sense Catholic, which, as the name itself and the reason of the thing declare, comprehends all universally. This rule we shall observe if we follow universality, antiquity, consent. We shall follow universality if we confess that one faith to be true, which the whole Church throughout the world confesses; antiquity, if we in no wise depart from those interpretations which it is manifest were notoriously held by our holy ancestors and fathers; consent, in like manner, if in antiquity itself we adhere to the consentient [unanimous] definitions and determinations of all, or at the least of almost all priests and doctors. (Ibid.)

This is where we get the phrase "unanimous consent of the fathers" as an expression of what is believed "everywhere, always, by all."

But of course, these phrases are all relative, because there are always exceptions; we can always cite one church where a particular doctrine was denied, or one period in history when it was called into question, or some doctor or even a saint who erred on a specific point. There is no unity of "everywhere, always, all," at least in an absolute sense. Given that fact, are we left with nothing beyond Chillingworth's opinion that the concept of "unanimous consent of the fathers" is ephemeral? Are we left with Chillingworth's conclusion that accepting Tradition means "popes against popes" and "councils against councils"?

Assuming we are not ready to grant Chillingworth's argument that there is no real unanimous consent of the fathers, while understanding that even a "unanimous" consent will not be so in an absolute sense, what can we make of St. Vincent's Canon? What does it mean practically speaking—how do we determine when something was kept by "the whole Church," and what does this mean?

In his masterful study on clerical celibacy, *The Apostolic Origins of Priestly Celibacy*, Fr. Christian Cochini proposes five criteria for applying the Vincentian Canon. The context in which Fr. Cochini discusses this problem has to do with priestly celibacy, but these considerations are applicable to the study of any issue where there is a question of patristic consensus.

1. A point of doctrine or discipline can be said to be kept by the whole Church at a given time in its history if the majority of men who enjoy great moral and intellectual authority in the Church during that age share the same opinions about it. In the early Church, we would be referring to the most influential Fathers, the most eminent doctors and renowned bishops, credited by their contemporaries and posterity with exceptional value. Thus we do not need the totality of all the opinions of the churchmen of that age; those who were most important serve as spokesmen for the rest.

2. A point of doctrine or discipline can be said to be kept by the whole Church at a given time in its history if it is kept by the apostolic churches; i.e., above all, those churches founded by the Apostles. This is what St. Irenaeus meant when he said that "it is in any church that it [the Tradition of the apostles] can be perceived by those who want to see the truth."[2] Again, it is not necessary to know the opinion of *every* apostolic church; just the opinions of the most important or more representative suffice, unless we have formal evidence to the contrary that other apostolic churches were in disagreement with them. For example, if we know Alexandria, Rome, and Antioch were in agreement on a certain point, but Corinth, Ephesus, and Philippi are silent, it is presumed these lesser apostolic churches are in agreement with the greater unless there is formal recorded testimony to the contrary.

3. A point of doctrine or discipline can be said to be kept by the whole Church at a given time in its history if

---

[2] St. Irenaeus, *Adversus Haereses*, III,2,1.

it is found to be kept by all the bishops; and what is kept by the bishops is expressed in the acts of their regional synods and episcopal assemblies where they met to come to common conclusions deemed to be in continuity with tradition. The North African synods of the third to the fifth centuries, the Gallic councils of the fifth century and the famed Spanish councils of the sixth and seventh centuries are excellent examples of such synods. Of course, episcopal consent is even more perfectly reflected in the judgments of ecumenical councils, both in what was decided at the time of these councils and in how later generations of bishops interpreted the decisions of these councils.

4. A point of doctrine or discipline can be said to be kept by the whole Church at a given time in its history if between that time and the apostolic age there is no decision coming from any authorized hierarchical authority attesting to the existence of a contrary belief or practice. This could only be the authority of an ecumenical council or the Holy See; the decisions of local synods would not be enough to affirm that something was "always maintained" in the universal Church since these synods are limited in scope of time and space. A great example of this is infant baptism. Despite the fact that it is not clearly attested until the 3rd century, there exists no authoritative opinions contrary to the practice from the apostolic age till that time. Therefore we presume such practices to be apostolic and held by the entire Church.

5. A point of doctrine or discipline can be said to be kept by the whole Church if during the same time the point in question was never contested in the name of a contrary tradition by any of the apostolic churches. If there was a dispute, it needs to be examined whether this led to the recognition of two parallel traditions (as in the Quartodeciman quarrel between Polycarp and Pope Anicetus) or to the rejection of one tradition, as in the case of the baptismal controversy between Pope Stephen and St. Cyprian, which was resolved in favor of the pope.

When the point in question is contested only by groups or individuals out of communion with the apostolic churches, the possibility of an unbroken tradition is not thereby called into question, as certain points of dogma are always questioned by heretics.

If we follow these principles in applying the Vincentian Canon, we see that we do not wind up with the dilemma Chillingworth proposed. Rather, as Newman explained in his famous *Essay*, we are able to delineate a clear and uniform testimony from antiquity running like a golden thread throughout the ages of the Church, providing a clear consensus as to what is and is not part of the Deposit of Faith. There is clearly no analogy between the very real dilemma of the disunity of Protestant sects and the alleged "popes against popes" accusation of Chillingworth.